Foreword

Welcome

For this tenth entry in the *Modelling British Railways* series, attention is turned away from locomotives and rolling stock subjects for the first time to look at infrastructure, specifically diesel depots. Such facilities remain a perennial favourite among modellers as they can be tailored to suit any size of layout and allow a collection of locos to be shown off to advantage.

The options for modelling depots have expanded greatly in recent years thanks to the emergence of 3D printing and laser cutting with a raft of small suppliers now offering kits for an assortment of different styles of depot buildings and ancillary structures, along with all sorts of detailing parts to bring that all important realism to a layout. Gone are the days of many depot layouts employing either the Hornby recreation of Ripple Lane or Peco's HST depot based on Bounds Green, with several of the main manufacturers also now marketing an assortment of suitable resin structures.

A successful depot layout is about more than just the main building though, and the aim of this publication is to look at all the aspects that make up a maintenance facility, be it from today or back in the British Rail era. As a result, fuelling facilities are considered in detail along with all the other structures that would be found, such as offices, stores buildings and even boiler houses.

Over the years, I have been fortunate enough to visit a number of depots, not just for open days but also press events and working on a preserved diesel, allowing numerous photos to be captured of subjects that are typically overlooked. For example, Old Oak Common was visited on many occasions during its final months of operation, allowing the depot facilities to be extensively photo-surveyed with hundreds of p̲ ̲ ̲ ̲ ̲ ̲en. Providing inspiration is therefore a key aim of this publication.

Another important aspect of diesel depots that should not be ignored is their operation, so this volume also considers how they were laid out to optimise movements and what facilities would be provided at each location to enable the desired level of maintenance to be carried out. Not every site performed maintenance though so basic stabling points are included too.

Thanks must go as ever to various people who have contributed towards this volume, including Ian Manderson, Clive Mortimore, and David Ratcliffe along with the other modellers and photographers credited throughout. Particular thanks are due to my father, Terry, for many of the modelling projects featured within these pages.

Simon Bendall
Editor

ABOVE: Having served as a locomotive maintenance facility for 103 years, the end was soon to come for the former Great Western Railway depot at Old Oak Common in order to make way for the new Crossrail tunnel lining segment production facility and ultimately the line's EMU maintenance depot. On March 28, 2009, 56096, 56081, 56071, and 56059 were all undergoing preparations in the legendary 'Factory' heavy repair workshop prior to being hauled away to either Crewe or Eastleigh for further storage two months later. All carry the grey livery of Fertis following use in France on construction trains for the TGV Est line. Simon Bendall

◁ COVER: Since privatisation, there has been a drive to concentrate maintenance on a core number of depots with much reduced facilities provided elsewhere. The fuelling shed now installed at Immingham is seen on March 17, 2021, with 60010 present. Craig Adamson

Modelling BR: Diesel Depots **3**

VISIT OUR ONLINE SHOP
shop.keypublishing.com/greatlayouts4

Key Shop

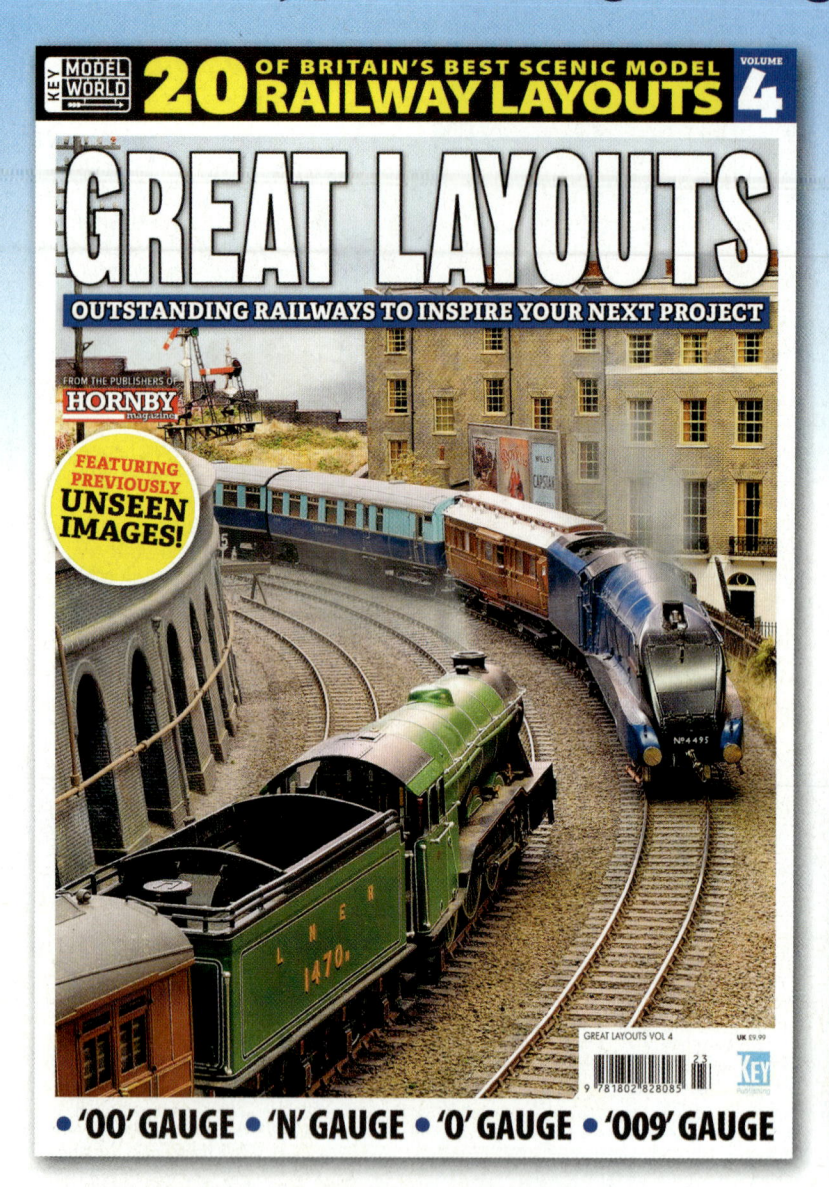

KEY MODEL WORLD
20 OF BRITAIN'S BEST SCENIC MODEL RAILWAY LAYOUTS VOLUME 4

GREAT LAYOUTS
OUTSTANDING RAILWAYS TO INSPIRE YOUR NEXT PROJECT

FROM THE PUBLISHERS OF **HORNBY** magazine

FEATURING PREVIOUSLY UNSEEN IMAGES!

• 'OO' GAUGE • 'N' GAUGE • 'O' GAUGE • '009' GAUGE

Hornby Magazine presents the fourth volume of its popular Great Layouts series bringing together some of the very best model railways to have ever featured in the magazine. In Great Layouts - Volume 4 we showcase 20 of Britain's most loved model railways, including magnum opus exhibition layouts such as the Gresley Beat and Shenston Road, plus behind-the-scenes with home-based layouts, including stunning recreations of Doncaster and Dent. Lavishly illustrated with the best photographs from the Hornby Magazine archive, each layout features previously unpublished material as we guide you through the story of their conception and construction.

Scan me to order!

ONLY £9·99 + FREE P&P*

SUBSCRIBERS don't forget to use your **£2 OFF DISCOUNT CODE!**

IF YOU ARE INTERESTED IN **MODEL RAIL** YOU MAY ALSO WANT TO ORDER...

MODELLING BRITISH RAILWAYS DIESEL DEPOTS — £8·99

MODELLING BRITISH RAILWAYS ENGINEERS WAGONS OF PRIVATISATION — £8·99

MODELLING BRITISH RAILWAYS MODERN FREIGHT LOCOMOTIVES — £8·99

MODELLING BRITISH RAILWAYS LOCOMOTIVES OF THE 1990s — £8·99

FREE P&P* when you order online at...
shop.keypublishing.com/greatlayouts4
Call +44 (0)1780 480404 (Monday to Friday 9am-5.30pm GMT)

Also available from **W.H Smith** and all leading newsagents.

*Free 2nd class P&P on all UK & BFPO orders. Overseas charges apply.

699/23

Contents

ABOVE: **Although now retired from the exhibition circuit, Western Road was a fine recreation of a Western Region diesel depot, recalling the spirit of the likes of Bristol Bath Road in the mid-1970s. Built by Mike Anson, the P4 gauge exhibit was normally seen running in 1976 condition with the last stragglers of the Class 52 'Westerns' succumbing to the Class 50 invasion. However, for this image, the layout had been temporarily backdated to the hydraulic era with guest appearances from part of the Canada Road fleet. With the latter being EM gauge, it was unfortunately only a static visit! Prominent in this view is Pete Johnson's D1059** *Western Empire*, **the 'thousand' being a re-worked Heljan model, while its companions include a Class 14, Class 22 and two 'Hymeks'.** Ian Manderson

- **6** Depot operations
- **14** Stabling points
- **22** Loco inspection points
- **28** Diesel depot development
- **66** Fuelling points
- **86** Ancillary structures
- **110** Internal users

ISBN: 978 1 80282 747 7
Editor: Simon Bendall
Senior editor, specials: Roger Mortimer
Email: roger.mortimer@keypublishing.com
Cover design: Steve Donovan
Design: SJmagic DESIGN SERVICES, India
Advertising Sales Manager: Brodie Baxter
Email: brodie.baxter@keypublishing.com
Tel: 01780 755131
Advertising Production: Becky Antoniades
Email: rebecca.antoniades@keypublishing.com

SUBSCRIPTION/MAIL ORDER
Key Publishing Ltd, PO Box 300, Stamford, Lincs, PE9 1NA
Tel: 01780 480404
Subscriptions email: subs@keypublishing.com
Mail Order email: orders@keypublishing.com
Website: www.keypublishing.com/shop

PUBLISHING
Group CEO: Adrian Cox
Publisher, Books and Bookazines:
Jonathan Jackson
Published by
Key Publishing Ltd, PO Box 100, Stamford, Lincs, PE9 1XQ
Tel: 01780 755131
Website: www.keypublishing.com

PRINTING
Precision Colour Printing Ltd, Haldane, Halesfield 1, Telford, Shropshire. TF7 4QQ

DISTRIBUTION
Seymour Distribution Ltd, 2 Poultry Avenue, London, EC1A 9PU
Enquiries Line: 02074 294000.

We are unable to guarantee the bona fides of any of our advertisers. Readers are strongly recommended to take their own precautions before parting with any information or item of value, including, but not limited to money, manuscripts, photographs, or personal information in response to any advertisements within this publication.

© Key Publishing Ltd 2023
All rights reserved. No part of this magazine may be reproduced or transmitted in any form by any means, electronic or mechanical, including photocopying, recording or by any information storage and retrieval system, without prior permission in writing from the copyright owner. Multiple copying of the contents of the magazine without prior written approval is not permitted.

Depot operations

Depot operations

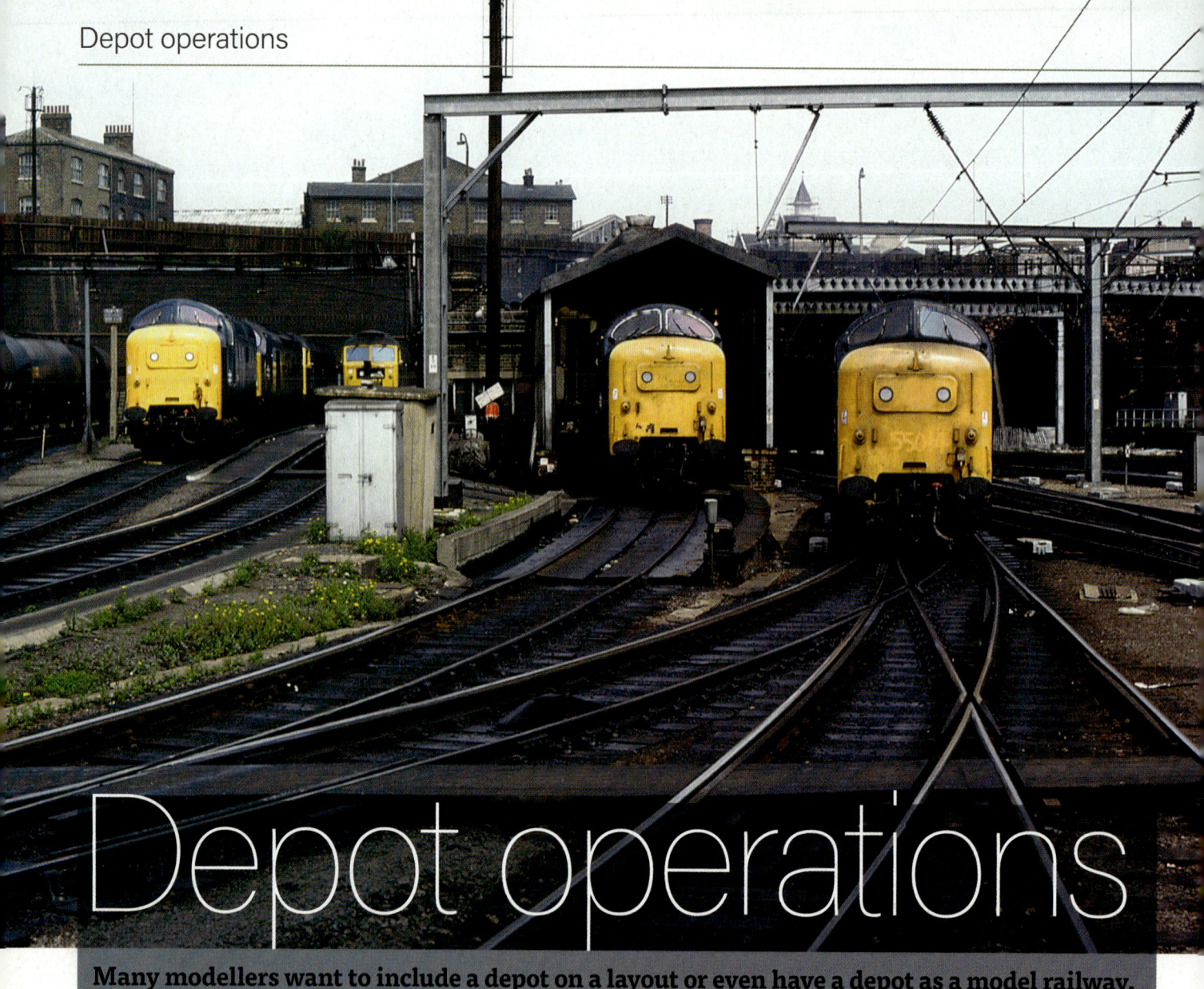

Many modellers want to include a depot on a layout or even have a depot as a model railway. However, such locations had a reason for existing and had a certain level of facilities available. Clive Mortimore describes what these were and how they can be applied in model form with the aid of trackplans, these being drawn by Jim Smith-Wright.

For there to be a depot at a location, there has to be a reason for it being there, such as the centre of a traffic flow or major junction. Some locations today do not seem as obvious to us as they were to the planers of the modernisation process in the 1960s. In fact, some diesel depots were built following old steam workings and were found to be in the wrong location and consequently under-used from very early on.

Depots were there to provide several functions. At some locations, all that was required was for somewhere the loco crews could sign on, while other locations were purely for the stabling of locos between duties. For modellers who wish to provide this level of provision, all that is required is a siding or two for the locos and a building which can be used as the drivers' lobby. During the 1960s and 1970s, some old steam sheds were utilised as covered accommodation for stabling locomotives without any other facilities.

When deciding on a diesel depot for a model railway, you will need to look at the level of maintenance you will be providing for your locos. This does not generally affect the basics of the trackplan, but it will help with setting your parameters. Using the 1986 designation codes for depots as a guide, I will endeavour to show how these can be applied to our model railways.

• Level one: Basically, this is a fuel point able to supply fuel, water, oil, sand and to carry out routine servicing. Some of these could be quite simple affairs, like Ranelagh Bridge, without any buildings but also included what on the surface looked like a higher-level depot with buildings. Old steam sheds often fell into this group.
• Level two: As above with the ability to carry out A and B examinations. Some diagrams would include the loco having its A exam at a fuelling point like Ranelagh Bridge so to differentiate between a Level one and Level two depot in model form would be quite difficult.
• Level three: These have covered accommodation with inspection pits along with lifting or jacking facilities. We are looking at a medium to large size depot, which in model form would be a layout on its own.
• Level four: These have the ability to carry out major work, including bogie and power unit changes. When built, many depots were not designed to perform power unit changes but have since been adapted to do so. This would be a depot of the size of Old Oak Common or Cardiff Canton.
• Level five. These are depots with fully equipped workshops for component exchange and body repairs. Some Western Region depots could undertake this type

ABOVE: The servicing depot alongside the throat of King's Cross station is a perfect example of a small scale locomotive maintenance facility being shoehorned into a very tight space. Despite this, it still featured a servicing shed with fuelling point, open air inspection pit, stabling sidings, and fuel storage tanks with adjacent tanker road. On May 12, 1979, 55014 *The Duke of Wellington's Regiment* needs a wash as it shunts across to the depot while classmates 55009 *Alycidon* and 55006 *The Fife & Forfar Yeomanry* look on in the company of a Class 40 and two Class 47s. The cramped conditions and lines laid on a gradient certainly made life interesting, but the depot was just five months from closure, the introduction of the HSTs making it redundant. Simon Bendall Collection

Depot operations

Table 1 – 1960s exam schedule			
Exam	Hours run between exams (real time)	Time taken to perform exam	Examination carried out
A	32-38 hours (2 days)	1 hour (2 man hours)	General service. Visual exam, test brakes and steam heating equipment where fitted.
B	125-150 hours (7-12 days)	6 hours (20 man hours)	More comprehensive service, checks on engine and running gear.
C	500-600 hours (Monthly)	8 hours (32 man hours)	As above plus change lubricating oil filters, clean air and fuel filters, clean radiators, check engine speed and running. Take lubricating oil sample for analysis.
D	1500-1800 hours (3 monthly)	16 hours (72 man hours)	As above. Check engine tappets. Remove and test fuel injectors. Examine regulator.
E	3000-3600 hours (6 monthly)	16 hours (96 man hours)	As above. Inspect engine camshafts. Check all control equipment and tighten connections.

of work due to the management's forward thinking, which included equipping them with heavy lifting equipment early on. Laira or Toton come into this class of depot.

Some depots had lower levels of work than the facilities installed suggested, this coming about due to changes in traffic patterns and rolling stock. For example, the introduction of the HSTs and spread of electrification both often had a detrimental effect on diesel depots in the areas concerned.

Workload
Maintenance schedules were worked out in conjunction with careful diagramming of locomotives, so they were at the right place for servicing and examination. With all the variables that still plague railway timetables, this naturally did not always happen as planned. Matters were greatly helped with the introduction of the TOPS computer system as the location of the loco was known, as well as when it was due for servicing. It could therefore be diagrammed so that it would be able to receive attention. Table 1 summarises the level of exam and the typical work to be carried out as devised in the 1960s. Over subsequent decades, changes were made to the exam cycle as technology advanced and new maintenance processes were developed. Table 2 relates to the servicing of Class 58s in the 1990s.

Most locos visiting a Traction Maintenance Depot (TMD) did so for a reason, even if it was for re-fuelling. If a loco was coming in for servicing or examination, it would be re-fuelled prior to anything else. Some locos coming in for an unscheduled repair would be shunted into a siding while awaiting a repair berth. There would be a few locos just coming on shed for stabling, normally shunters and locos working empty coaching stock trains. On a model, it is a fairly safe bet to run most locos onto the fuelling point on entering the depot.

From a Modern Railways article in 1967, the amount of work done by Toton for a four-week period was 1410 locos fuelled and 748 locos either serviced or repaired. This comprised 260 A exams, 194 B exams, 82 C exams, 40 D exams and 17 E exams. This leaves 155 locos that were repaired without being scheduled for servicing. The article goes on to list a total of 353 repairs and modifications to locos but does not state how many locos had more than one repair, nor the number of faults found on examination. To fuel a loco would take some time. For example, the fuel pumps at Tinsley delivered fuel at 50 gallons per minute while a Class 47 had a tank capacity of 850 gallons. Fuelling was normally done at the same time as the A exam, along with other servicing and restoring the levels of water, sand, and oil. This was a sample taken in the 1960s, but I doubt this pattern has changed very much since then.

Card operation
Using these figures as a basis, a modeller could build into their operating plan a means of representing these exams, thereby giving a greater level of realism. For example, two out of five locos coming onto the depot would be serviced, the level of facilities modelled determining how this was portrayed. If there was a separate servicing shed, then the A and B exams would be undertaken in this building, if not they may take place on the fuelling point.

If there were more substantial maintenance facilities, then some of the roads would be for the higher-level exams and others for repairs. This would be represented by more frequent exchanges of locos on one or two roads in the shed than the others. Looking at percentages, every 20th loco arriving would have a C exam, every 40th a D exam and every 100th an E exam. Every 10th loco would be an unscheduled repair and of the locos in for examination, one quarter would be found to need a repair. Repairs could be sub-divided into light and heavy and shed roads should be allocated accordingly.

Various methods could be used to decide which locos are due for exams and repairs and to what level in order to give a randomness to the operation of a layout and generate more 'play value'. One method would be to draw a card for each loco coming onto the depot which, using the above figures for Toton, would mean 100 cards. These would be divided as follows: 58 re-fuel only, three re-fuel and needing unscheduled light repair, one re-fuel and needing unscheduled heavy repair, 27 A or B exam, three A or B exam and light repair, six C exam, two D exam, one D exam and heavy repair, one E exam, one light repair not being re-fuelled

ABOVE: Like the servicing depot at King's Cross, Ranelagh Bridge catered for the immediate needs of locos working out of Paddington and saved the six-mile round trip to Old Oak Common. Opened in 1907, it once boasted a turntable and coaling facilities in addition to the water tower still standing on the left of the shot. Again compact in nature, it had by this June 1973 image been reduced to a fuelling and light servicing point. On this occasion, three Class 47s equipped with electric train heating gang up on a solitary 'Western', while tankers and stores wagons are also present. Simon Bendall Collection

Depot operations

Table 2 – 1990s Class 58 exam schedule		
Exam	**Hours run between exams (real time)**	**Examination carried out**
Fuel point or service check	Once a day to once every five days depending on diagram	Similar to the old A exam.
A	80 hours	As above. More comprehensive service, checks on engine and running gear. Take lubricating oil sample for analysis.
B	400 hours	As above. Change lubricating oil filters, clean air and fuel filters. Clean radiators. Check AWS and batteries. This takes eight hours.
C	1200 hours	A more detailed exam lasting 16 hours.
D	3600 hours	A more detailed exam, including changing of fuel injectors, checking the air compressors, traction motors and suspension.
F1	7200 hours	This is part of the component exchange maintenance system, where items are renewed, and the old ones go to a main works for reconditioning.
F2	14400 hours	As above but includes components with a longer service life.

ABOVE: The new diesel depot at Laira was an essay in concrete construction when completed in 1964, boasting some of the most comprehensive maintenance facilities to be found on the region. Five years after opening, a Warship and two Westerns lurk in the shadows of the fuelling area with the servicing shed behind. Looming over them is the heavy repair shed with the staff block to the left. Simon Bendall Collection

and, finally, one heavy repair not being re-fuelled.

To this could be added a few stabling only cards for both shunters and main line locos on local trip workings and stock duties. Shuffle the set of cards and as each loco enters the depot, turn over the top card to reveal what action you as depot manger/foreman have to take in respect to berthing the loco.

In practice
For my own depot layout, a set of 100 cards would be too unwieldy, therefore I use a pack of ordinary playing cards. Red cards are for locos going off depot and black for those coming on. On arrival, the loco halts outside the shunter's hut and he directs it to the fuel point or siding. If the card is a two of spades, then it is a shunting loco coming on for stabling purposes only, while a two of clubs is a shunter, Type 1 or Type 2 on trip or empty stock workings for stabling only; these all by-pass the fuelling point. A three, four, five or six are re-fuel only and go to the fuel line, seven is for double-headed locos for fuel only, and eight and nine for an A exam at the fuel point. Drawing a ten or a picture card requires a loco to go into covered accommodation for an exam or repair. A king indicates a loco that has to go for heavy repair or an E exam.

When moving locos on to the stabling loops, I refer back to the last black card; a spade means the loco will be stabled on number one or number three loop, while a club indicates loops two and four. This portrays the shed foreman preparing the locos for their next duties.

Red cards are for locos going off shed, a diamond from roads one or three and a heart for lines two and four. If done correctly, one road out of each pair is filling up with locos while the other is emptying, ensuring a turnover of locos. Picture cards not only release a loco from one of the storage loops but also a loco from the shed, with the latter normally placed on the storage loops before departing the depot entirely later on. Completing the cards, aces and jokers are for movements of the fuel tankers, stores vehicles, snowploughs, and breakdown train.

Using dice is another way to introduce some operational fun to a depot layout by again regulating which locos are stabled, serviced and repaired. I would use two dice together with the first role determining if a loco is going on or off shed, a two to a six could be an off shed movement, eight to 12 on shed and a seven would again be for fuel tankers, stores and the like. For the locos coming on depot, a second role of two to seven would be re-fuel and stable, eight and nine A and B exams, ten a C exam or repair, 11 a D exam and 12 an E exam. For locos coming off depot, role again and if the score is the same this would release a repaired loco from the shed.

Depots perform an essential role and we as modellers do tend to forget that loco crews also needed servicing, so they need some form of accommodation. Larger depots would have a canteen for the staff that worked at the depot as well.

Allocation and diagrams
Another factor dictating the size of a depot is the number of diagrams needing to be covered. Table 3 shows the number of steam, diesel and shunting locos allocated to the Eastern Region in 1965. If you compare the number of diagrams to the allocation, it can be seen there is spare capacity, which is taken up by locos in works, under repair at depots or receiving one of the longer examinations.

Looking at Finsbury Park, there would be 43 main line diesel locos not diagrammed to work each day along with six shunters. Not all of these would be at the depot at the same time but for a shed of Finsbury Park's size, it could have about 30 locos present during the day, of which 18 could be serviced and repaired under cover. From memory, about half of the locos seen at Finsbury Park on visits were in the open, so 30 would be about right. These would be parked in appropriate positions to minimise the amount of shunting required to release a loco, which was only achieved with careful planning.

Using Table 3 as an indicator, a shed with 45 main line diagrams would have an allocation of about 60 locos, of which a minimum of 12 would be on the depot at any one time. Of these, up to five or six would be under some sort of cover being repaired or examined.

Depot operations

Depot	Steam locos	Main line diesels	Diesel shunters	Main line diesel & steam loco diagrams	Shunter diagrams
Stratford		122	54	94	40
Parkston			17		13
Cambridge			13		10
March		52	23	46	19
Norwich		30	21	20	18
Ipswich		53	13	35	8
Finsbury Park		163	31	120	25
Hitchin			12		11
New England	3		25		21
Doncaster	61		20	60	17
Frodingham	42		11	40	10
Retford	32		10	35	9
Lincoln		7	9	6	6
Immingham	36	7	39	30	26
Colwick	49		25	44	15
Canklow	37			31	
Tinsley		158	38	70	29
Darnell			43		40
Wath		40	12	61	9
Langwith	45		10	43	8
Barrow Hill	39		38		
Staveley	30		22		

Table 3 - Eastern Region allocations and diagrams 1965

For shunters, a requirement for 25 diagrams would mean an allocation of 30 and of these, a minimum of four could be at their home shed. Add a few locos being re-fuelled between diagrams and the depot becomes fairly busy. At weekends and overnight, many more locos would be on shed between diagrams. In contrast, today's loco fleets are much more tightly diagrammed thanks, in part, to better reliability and also a desire to keep costs to a minimum so depots have far fewer spare locos sitting about.

A basic plan

Once you have worked out the level of maintenance work you wish to provide and its allocation, you can begin to work out a depot's size. This then influences the track layout with several small and medium sized depots described here.

As already stated, most locos coming onto a depot would be re-fuelled so, in the case of a change of diagram, they would be ready to take over the duty. From the fuelling point, they would be stabled or moved into the shed building. To reduce the number of conflicting movements, most diesel sheds had a flow pattern. Taking the trackplan of Ranelagh Bridge stabling point, outside Paddington, as a basis, I will try to describe how this all fits into place, see Figure 1.

On entering the stabling point, a loco would move onto one of the fuelling points, and if it were due an A exam while being serviced, it would be parked on the road with the inspection pit. Both fuel roads could only take two locos so, if both roads were in use, a loco would join the queue. After being serviced, the loco would move onto headshunt A, and from there it would reverse to headshunt B. Moving onto headshunt B keeps the double slip at the entrance of the sidings clear for locos coming on or going off shed.

From headshunt B, the loco would be reversed into one of the stabling sidings. The placement of locos in such sidings to prevent too much shunting when the loco

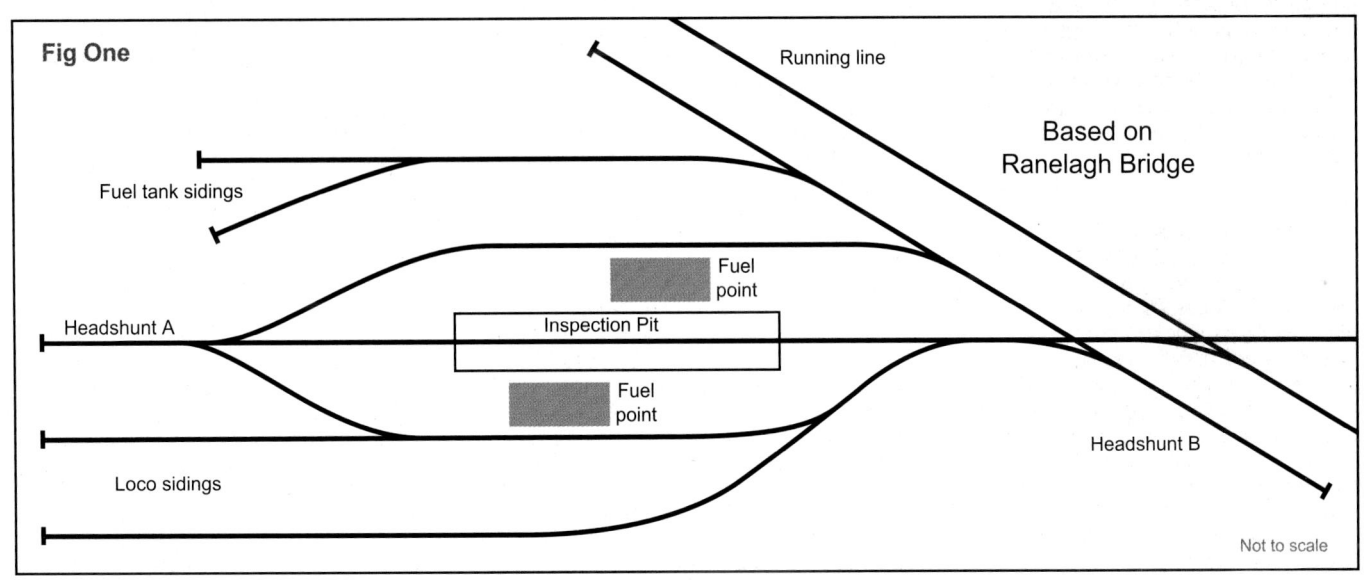

Fig One — Based on Ranelagh Bridge

Running line, Fuel tank sidings, Headshunt A, Fuel point, Inspection Pit, Fuel point, Headshunt B, Loco sidings

Not to scale

Modelling BR: Diesel Depots 9

Depot operations

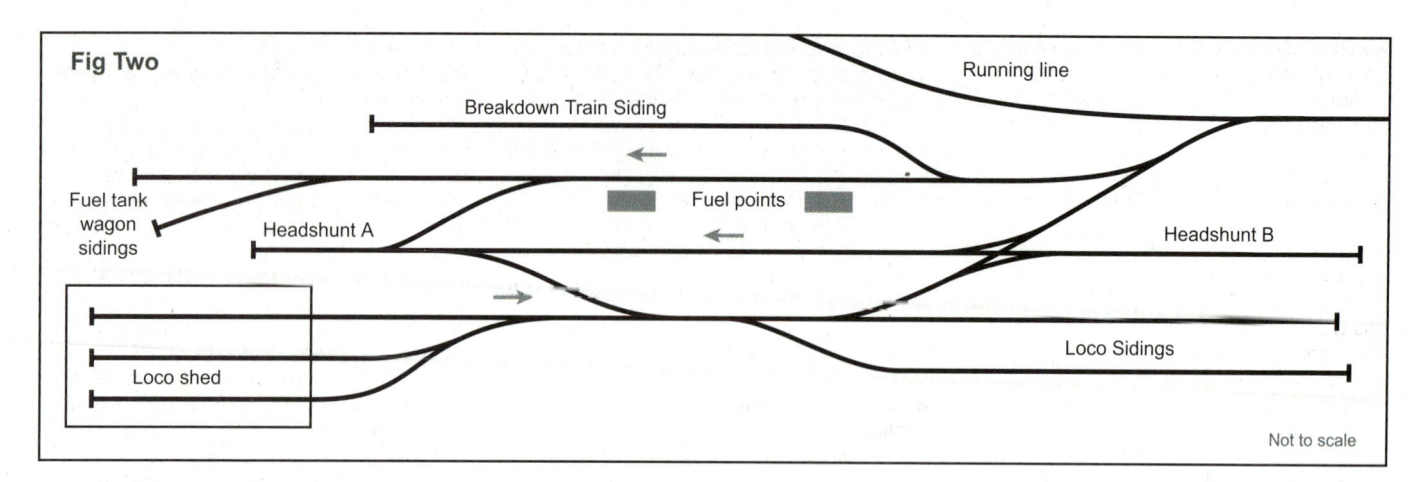

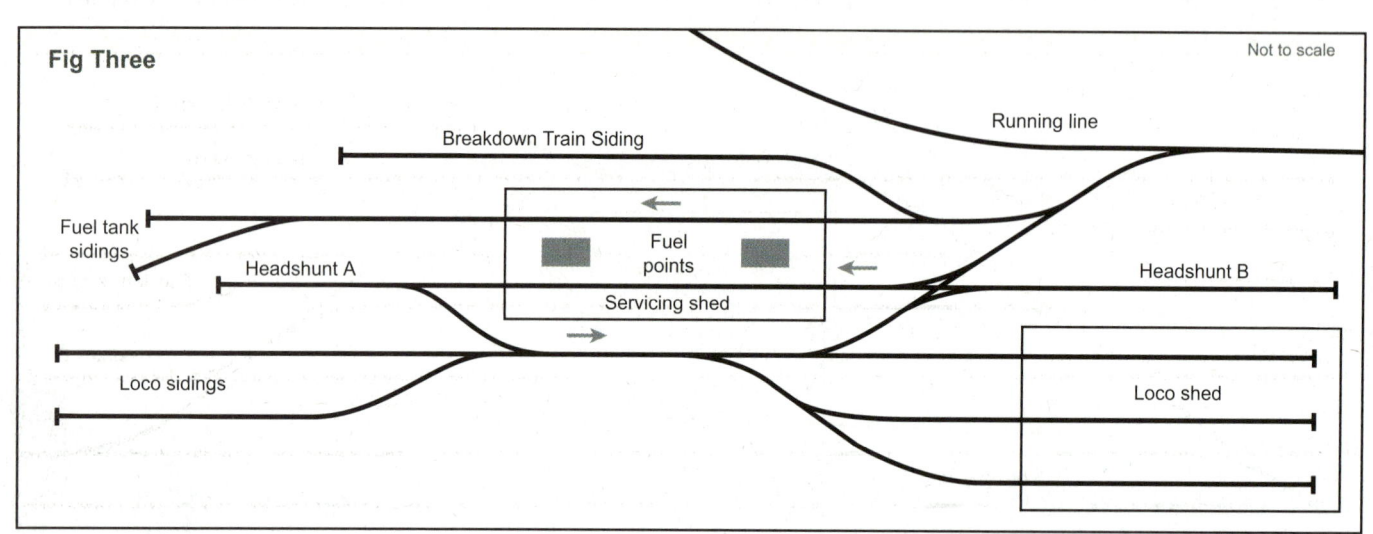

Fig Two

- Running line
- Breakdown Train Siding
- Fuel tank wagon sidings
- Headshunt A
- Fuel points
- Headshunt B
- Loco shed
- Loco Sidings

Not to scale

Fig Three

Not to scale

- Running line
- Breakdown Train Siding
- Fuel tank sidings
- Headshunt A
- Fuel points
- Servicing shed
- Headshunt B
- Loco sidings
- Loco shed

ABOVE: **The stabling sidings at Toton play host to 56016, 47198 and an unidentified Class 45/0 in June 1985 with a Class 31 doing its best to hide in the background. The ground conditions are typical of a BR depot at the time with oil soaked ballast, hand points and some signage. Large depots would often collect withdrawn locos for use as spares donors, but it was less common to see them grounded, as in the case of 'Peak' 45054.** Simon Bendall Collection

Depot operations

was due to exit the shed was quite an art; on a layout this is not a problem as we tend to like shunting our locos. Keeping to the flow pattern also reduces the possibility of accidents within the depot area.

Notice that Ranelagh Bridge has all the basic features of a TMD, including servicing roads, fuel tanker sidings and loco storage sidings. Depending on the level of maintenance to be performed and the predicted number of locos using the depot, this would determine the final size, amount of covered work area and number of loco sidings. At larger depots, there would be additional sidings for a breakdown train, stores wagons and snowploughs.

The delivery of fuel tankers and the removal of the empties would be done with the minimal disruption to the shed workings. At many depots, the fuel would be delivered on a trip working by a shunter. In order to position the loco at the right end of the train to either shunt the wagons or for it to make the return working, it would need to use a depot's run round loop, which was often formed of one of the fuel roads and the return road. This would be made more interesting if a brake van was required to be added! Rail delivery of other stores and lubricating oil would cause similar problems, as would the return of the breakdown crane and its support coaches from a duty. Before leaving Ranelagh Bridge, a note about locos leaving a depot. The driver would advance to the exit signal, telephone the signal box, and inform the signalman that the loco was ready to depart.

Mid-sized options

Moving up in size, Figure 2 retains the basic principles that are found in Ranelagh Bridge but with the addition of some extra sidings, including one for a breakdown train, and a maintenance shed. The two fuelling points have been relocated onto the same road, which allows up to four locos to be serviced at one time.

In Figure 3, the positions of the loco shed and stabling sidings have been swapped, while a servicing shed has been added over the fuelling points. The practice of having a servicing shed varied from region to region but could be found at depots on all of them.

There were some locations, such as Burton-upon-Trent, Ripple Lane, and Colchester, where the only building was

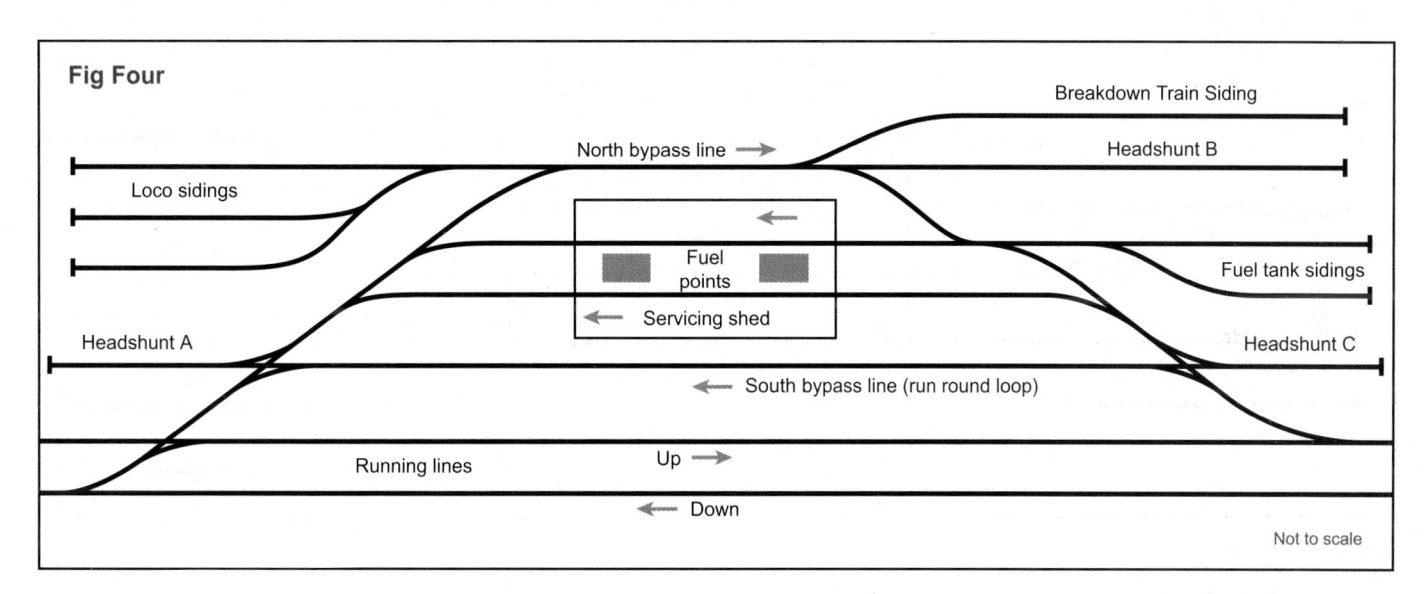

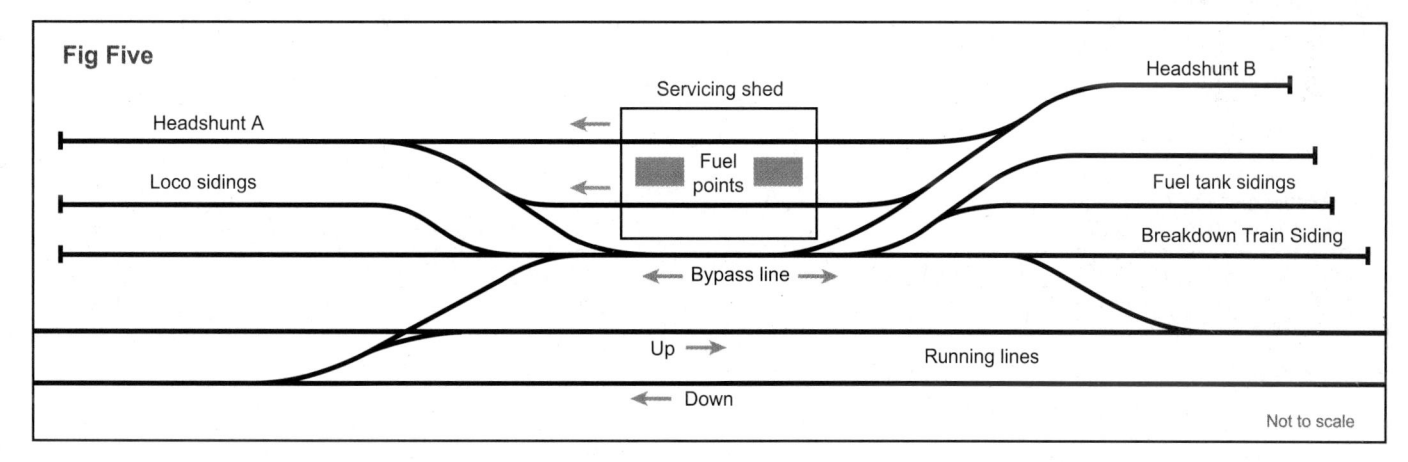

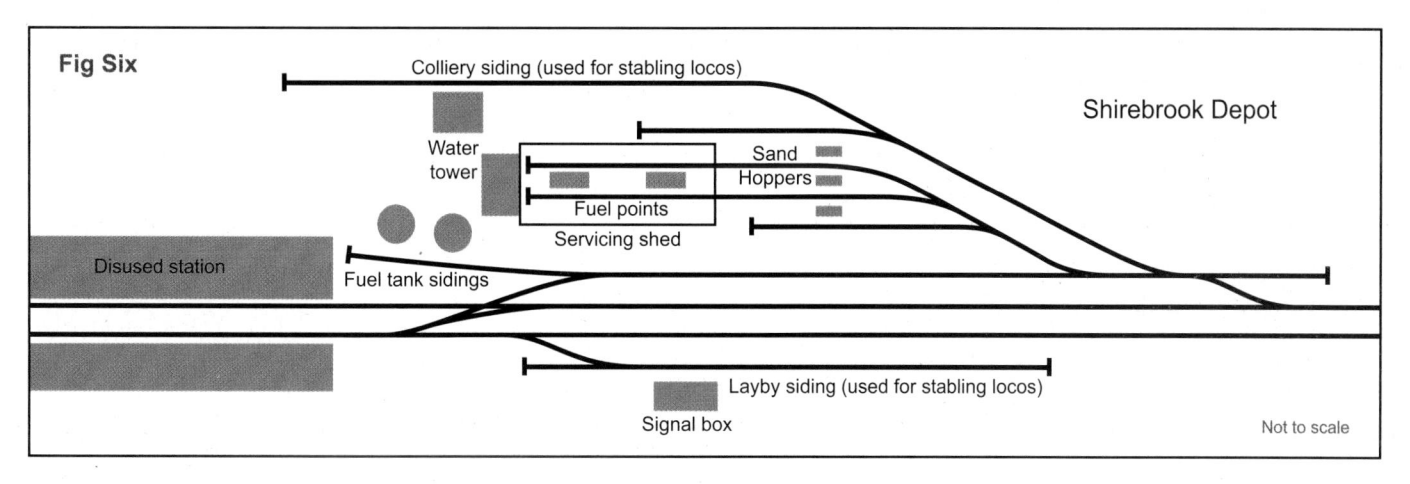

Depot operations

ABOVE: With the Glasgow skyline as a backdrop, a fine array of Scottish motive power was residing on Eastfield TMD in July 1990. On the left of the shot is 37402 *Oor Wullie* with 26038 behind, while also identifiable are large logo blue 47644 *The Permanent Way Institution* and a de-named 20118, the former Thornaby favourite having not long moved north of the border. Eastfield was another well equipped depot, capable of performing heavy lifts alongside all the daily maintenance, fuelling and servicing tasks. Like several other large depots, it was also responsible for maintaining the local Diesel Multiple Unit (DMU) fleet so complete sets and odd cars mixed with the locos, giving further modelling options. Simon Bendall Collection

the servicing shed. In Figure 4, I have moved things around but retained the basic principles. A loco coming off the up line would reverse onto the fuel point, then onto headshunt A, reverse to headshunt B and then again onto the loco sidings.

A fuel tanker train entering from the up line could be shunted into place by three routes, one onto the south bypass line, headshunt A then onto the fuel sidings via the north bypass line. Route two would be to reverse onto the north bypass line and then run-round, while the third option would be to reverse onto the down line and shunt onto the north bypass line. This would also be the route used for fuel trains coming on shed from the down line. Locos coming off shed on to the up line simply exit the depot, while those going on to the down line would do so via headshunt C and the south bypass line.

Where space was at a premium, the bypass line could be bi-directional as seen in Figure 5. For the fuel train loco to run round its train, it would either have to use the running lines or go through the servicing shed, the former being more likely. Not all locations had the fuelling points on a loop, some were on dead end sidings instead, such as Shirebrook and the St Pancras stabling point at Cambridge Street.

Shirebrook depot, as shown in Figure 6, used the old station goods yard as its site. When first built, it had Eastern Region elevated sand hoppers outside the shed building. I am not sure when these features were removed but they had gone by the 1980s, while re-fuelling took place in the servicing shed. Any running round the fuel tankers would have involved the running lines.

A model example

For my own depot layout of Hanging Hill (see Figure 7), which is based on Eastern Region practice, locos arriving on shed go to the fuel points then headshunt A, before reversing onto the centre road. From here, they can either go to headshunt C for stabling on one of the loops or to the loco shed.

Stabling loops have an obvious advantage over dead end sidings as locos do not get trapped on the bufferstops. With dead end sidings, I found that locos at the far end did not move at all during an operating session

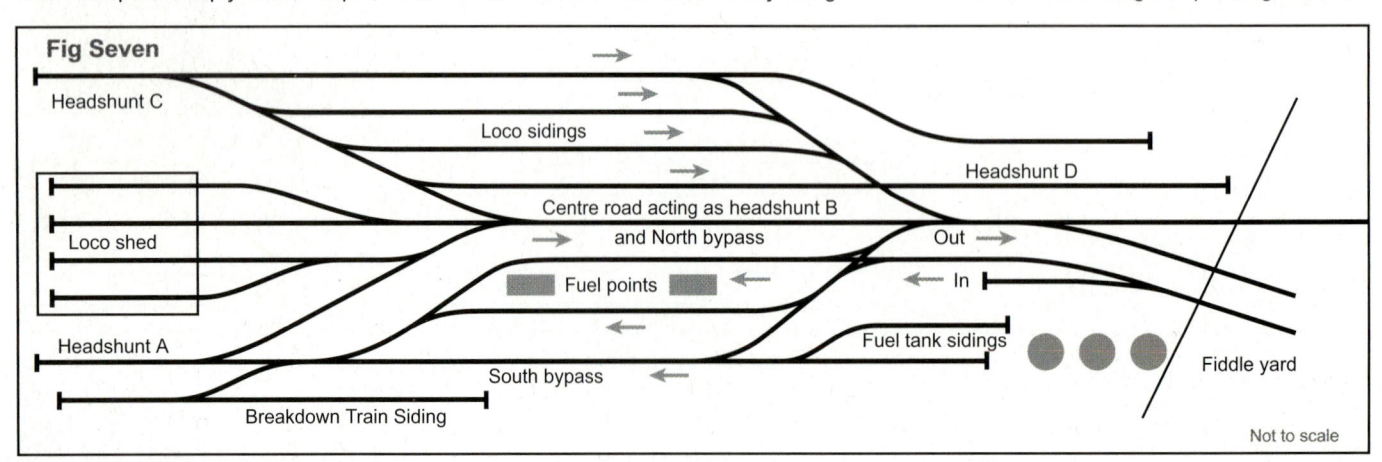

Fig Seven

Not to scale

12 www.keymodelworld.com

Depot operations

unless I made an effort and shunted lots of locos. With the loop system, I fill up from one end of two loops as I empty from the other two. When full, I revert back to the two that have been emptied by using the card system described above. I have found this makes sure that all my locos get a run during an exhibition. Headshunt D is for any shuffling of locos that may be required for diagramming purposes.

In real life, shed length could at times be a problem. At Finsbury Park, the single-ended shed roads each accommodated three locos but if the one at the inner end was to be released, then work had to stop on the other two locos so they could be shunted out of the way. All other Eastern Region sheds where only two locos long as a consequence, making loco release somewhat easier.

While on the subject of siding length, headshunt and fiddle yard lengths should be included in the calculations before building the depot. I begin by working out the maximum length of train for the fiddle yard. For Hanging Hill, this is three 15ft wheelbase tank wagons, a brake van, and a shunting locomotive, which is just under 24 inches.

Locomotive lengths govern another maximum, so I work on the basic length being a Class 40 or 'Deltic'. On my previous depot layout, Pig Lane, the headshunts were one 'basic loco' long but on Hanging Hill, which is much larger, each headshunt can take two 'basic loco' lengths. Another factor to consider is the amount of overhang, both end and central, that would cause moving locos to hit stationary ones.

I have found that laying out your layout in paper form, be it Peco templates or templates of the points I intend to use, on a sheet of wallpaper enables me to assess if everything is going to fit in the space parameters I have. By placing a couple of Class 40s on the pencil line representing the siding and then using a third Class 40 for end overhang and a Western for central overhang, I can check that there is enough clearance. 'Westerns' mathematically should not have the most central overhang, this should be the prerogative of the 'Deltics', but not in 4mm scale for some strange reason. In some cases, I make sidings four inches longer than the two 'basic loco' lengths, which allows a wagon, snowplough, or brake tender to occupy the end without affecting the usage of the siding.

Unless DCC is going to be used then storage sidings need to have isolating sections on them. Too many diesel depots fail to get the sidings right because they make the isolating sections the length of the longest loco. It looks unrealistic in 4mm when a two-foot loco siding has only two shunters on, and they are not buffer-to-buffer. I work on the basis that a Class 40 is just under 12 inches long while a Class 23 'Baby Deltic' is eight inches, and a shunter is four inches. Dividing a siding into four inch sections means that any combination of loco classes can share the same siding; a '40' needs three sections switched off, a 'Baby Deltic' two and so on. Classes like the '31s' and '37s', which are approximately ten inches, may need two or three sections depending on the other occupants of the sidings.

I was told by an ex-Stratford driver that the reason locos are stabled buffer to buffer is that when stopping your loco there is so much oil on the track that it just slides until hitting the 100 tons of diesel loco parked in front. From experience, the isolating sections for fuelling points are best set at the length of your longest loco as there will only ever be one loco to a pump. Getting the basics right in depot design can turn what would otherwise be a random collection of stabled locos into a well observed depot worth exhibiting and viewing.

ABOVE: A number of former steam sheds were turned over to maintaining diesel traction during the 1960s, many of the larger depots being ultimately rebuilt to better suit the needs of the newcomers. Eastfield is seen again on August 24, 1969, shortly before the original depot was demolished and rebuilt as illustrated on the previous page. Standing over an external pit is re-engined Class 29 6121 in the company of a Class 47 and, inside the shed, a Class 20.
Simon Bendall Collection

Stabling points

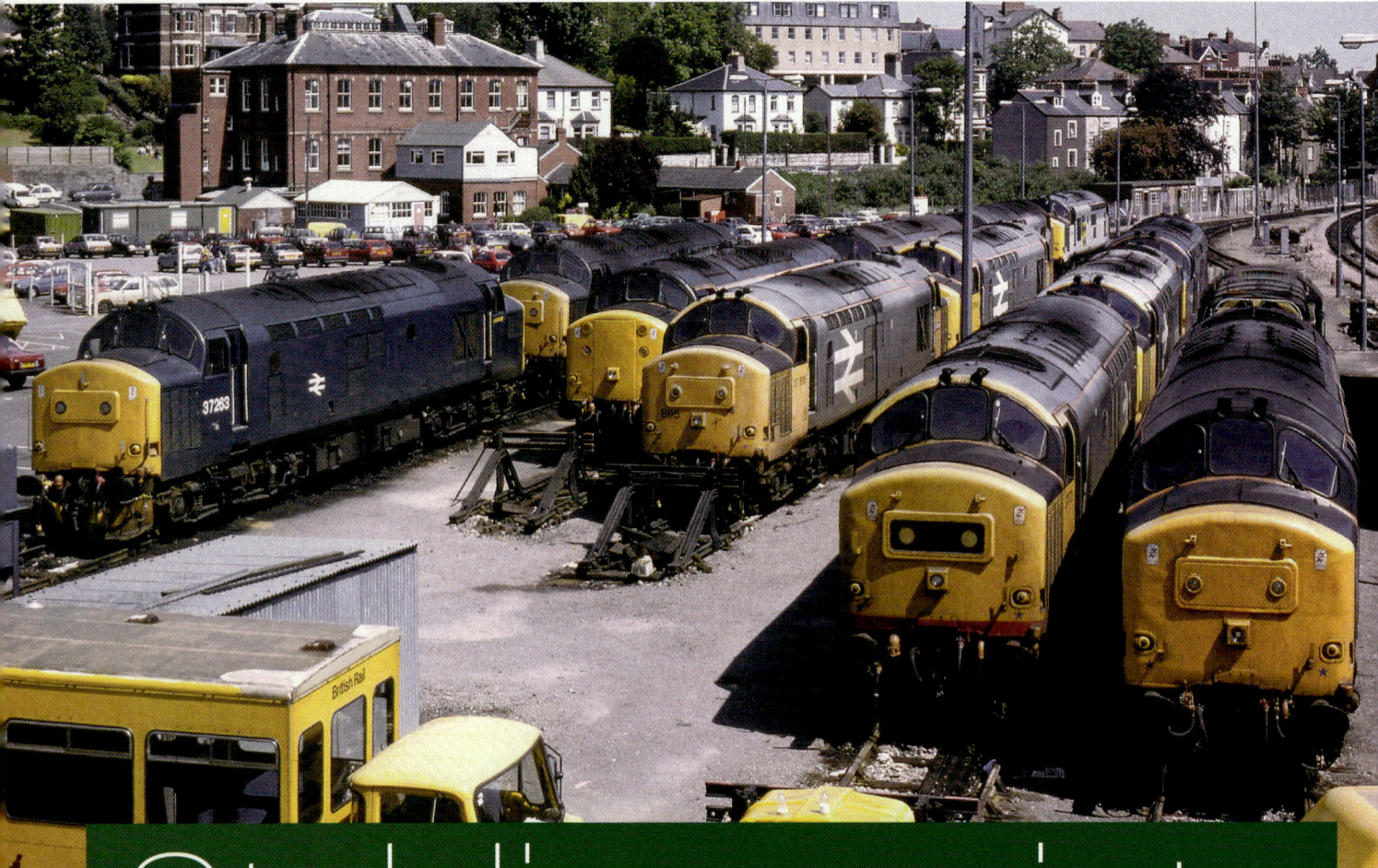

Stabling points

The smallest form of 'depot' offered no maintenance facilities whatsoever, being simply one or more sidings that could be used to stable locos between duties or at weekends. Found in all manner of situations, Simon Bendall looks at some examples.

Stabling points have long served a variety of purposes, invariably being somewhere locos can park up, or stable in railway parlance, out of the way to await their next duty, be it later the same day or over a weekend. Typically, they amount to two or three sidings, sometimes less, sometimes more, in either a dead end configuration or as loops. Typically, no maintenance facilities are provided whatsoever, although lighting and some form of walking route may be found.

Most large stations had somewhere within their environs to stable one or more locos, even if it was just the resident shunter, be it an otherwise redundant bay platform, short spur, or a fan of sidings. At terminus stations, these held spare locos waiting their turn to take out passenger services or overnight mail and parcels trains. Locos assigned to trip empty coaching stock from the station platforms to a depot a few miles away could also be found.

If a station was a regular location for loco changes, such as electrics giving way to diesels, then a little more space may be afforded, allowing one type to be removed and stabled without blocking its replacement in. Unsurprisingly, as British Rail moved towards fixed formation trainsets and increasing numbers of multiple units, the need for locos to be kept around stations diminished rapidly, something not helped by a decline in mail traffic.

For freight locos, stabling points were found at or near to major traffic centres, be it yards or important customer terminals. Locos that did not need to return to a depot for fuel, repairs or exams therefore remained close at hand and often with some form of traincrew accommodation nearby to allow for booking on and off.

A stabling point is therefore the simplest form of loco facility to model and is perfect for a small layout, just requiring two or three sidings and a couple of points at the most basic level. If more space is available, stabling loops could be modelled to increase operational interest and prevent locos becoming trapped on the bufferstops. With some careful planning, part of a terminus station could also be portrayed by strategic use of retaining walls and other scenic breaks, locos sometimes being stabled in all manner of nooks and crannies. The following photos give a flavour of what was to be found and could be adapted easily enough to suit a small layout.

ABOVE: During the 1960s, Newport Godfrey Road sidings was home to a loco fuelling point and stabling sidings, the former eventually being decommissioned and demolished with the space partly given over to the signal and telegraph engineers. In 1987, the S&T compound was closed, and the stabling point re-laid with five sidings, all for loco use but with no facilities. In this form, Godfrey Road became quite celebrated for sights like this on June 18, 1989, where 37263, 37895 and 37372 repose in the sun with nine other Class 37s and a solitary Class 08. Located next to Newport station, the movements on and off the stabling point entertained enthusiasts until closure in 2006. Geoff Cann

Stabling points

RIGHT: **During the BR corporate era, locos engaged on coal traffic in southwest Wales congregated at Pantyffynnon at weekends to be stabled alongside the otherwise quiet station. This typically included two Class 08s assigned to local trip workings and a number of Class 37s, these often bringing brake vans with them. In June 1983, 08662 is prominent on the stabling point with three of the English Electric Type 3s. The 12-ton shoc-van was a permanent resident and is pictured in a later chapter.**
Simon Bendall Collection

LEFT: **Most terminus stations under BR had one or two spots that spare locos could be squirrelled away, usually in lesser used but more interesting parts, and Waterloo was no exception. Before they disappeared under the international platforms, the north side of the station had stabling sidings and a loading platform, this latter line also giving access to the lift for the Waterloo and City cars. During June 1988, 50032** *Courageous* **was to be found stabled here along with a Class 33/0, the office blocks offering potential for a backscene.**
Simon Bendall Collection

ABOVE: **A former haunt of the editor, Didcot was a wonderful place to spend a few hours in the late 1990s and early 2000s with the various local traffics ensuring plenty of action. As a result, the two stabling loops alongside the station often contained a variety of traction laying over and April 1, 1995, was no exception. Leading the line-up is tatty Railfreight Distribution-liveried 47283** *Johnnie Walker*, **which was soon to move to Freightliner, while the rest of the locos were now under Mainline Freight ownership. From right to left are 37072, 37065, 60073** *Cairn Gorm*, **37010 and 60079** *Foinaven*, **the two Class 60s having lost their sub-sector logos but still awaiting Mainline decals. Sadly, Didcot is rarely as interesting nowadays.** Anthony Kay

Modelling BR: Diesel Depots **15**

Stabling points

LEFT: Most large marshalling yards have typically had a set of sidings that are used for loco stabling, as exemplified by Mossend Up Loco Holding Sidings on April 5, 2016. On this occasion, they were particularly full with Freightliner Class 86s, including 86605 and 86610, waiting to work evening trains off the nearby Coatbridge container terminal, while the Class 66s, including 66598, were in the area for use on an engineering blockade at Glasgow Queen Street. Also present were GBRf's 92018 in Caledonian Sleeper teal and Royal Mail EMU 325015, which would also work south from Shieldmuir to Willesden overnight.
Adrian Nicholls

RIGHT: While the number of stabling locations has decreased drastically with privatisation, some have remained traditional hotspots of activity. Eastleigh, like Didcot, could be readily observed from the station and often featured GB Railfreight motive power. On August 7, 2015, 73201 *Broadlands*, 73107 and 66733 *Cambridge PSB* head for the yard on the other side of the overbridge as they pass 66757 *West Somerset Railway* and Colas interlopers 60095 and 60056. Since GBRf displaced DB as the operator of the yard, locos have tended to stable there rather than alongside the station.
John Dedman

ABOVE: If Eastleigh has declined in recent years, Tonbridge West Yard remains an excellent alternative to watch GBRf locos at work and rest, the footbridge over the yard providing great views of the predominately infrastructure traffic. Locos have traditionally stabled at this end of the yard, where the staff accommodation is, and on July 23, 2015, a recently rebuilt 73963 *Janice* has 73128 *OVS Bullied CBE* and, once again, BR blue-liveried 73201 *Broadlands* for company. Jim Ramsay

16 www.keymodelworld.com

York – a layout inspiration

Looking for an easily manageable OO gauge exhibition layout, Nick Gurney was inspired to create The Sidings, a modern day stabling point that draws heavily on the location found alongside York station. Model photos by John Humphries.

With experience of building two medium-sized exhibition layouts, I was looking for something much smaller and easier to both transport and operate for my next project, a maximum length of five feet being deemed optimal. At about this time, Tim Horn's laser cut baseboards came onto the market, which are a great idea as I particularly dislike making my own baseboards! I duly selected a set of the 65cm by 30cm scenic/photo 'plank' board kits.

These normally consist of three boards, namely a right hand end, left hand end and a middle. However, I opted for two right hand ends, one of which was turned round to make a fiddle yard on the left hand end of the layout. The boards come as a flat-pack kit and being laser cut, they fit together perfectly - you even get the bolts and wing nuts to join them together with just wood glue required.

With the baseboards being only a foot wide, I did not want to cram too much track onto them. As I had a lot of DRS locos, this was the theme I opted to model. Having always been interested in depot layouts, this was the obvious way to go but incorporating a servicing shed would take up too much space, so I settled instead on a stabling point.

Initially, I considered having three sidings but with two points required, the length of the sidings would be reduced. I then came across some photos on the internet of DRS locos stabled at York's former parcels sidings. Sited alongside the southern end of the station, these two sidings had been shortened and refurbished for stabling locos working in the area, DRS being one of their main users.

There were also some interesting aspects, such as Rawie friction bufferstops and two ground position signals.

Extra details

The 'modern scene in a small space' is the tag line I use for the layout, so I wanted to incorporate current day features that you do not often see modelled. Although now produced by Accurascale, the Rawie friction bufferstops were not available at the time, these being scratchbuilt for me by a friend who usually works with model boats. He came to the rescue again as I wanted a GSM-R radio mast, which incorporates part of an Express Models yard tower with the rest being scratchbuilt.

Another item not often seen modelled are electrical relay cabinets with the doors open. These make a nice cameo with two maintenance staff attired in hi-viz clothing working on them. Also added were cable trunking and the associated cables along with electric point heaters. The final major piece of infrastructure was two modern ground position signals, which came from the excellent range of colour light signals produced by Absolute Aspects. Other small scenic details added to complete the scene included some old rail lying around, tufts of grass and bushes, a discarded car hub-cap, traffic cones, a tyre, and a few birds.

It is not the most challenging layout to operate as it is just a case of shuttling locos on and off the stabling sidings with the occasional visit from the Network Rail inspection saloon *Caroline* or the Class 950 track recording DMU. All of the locos are sound fitted with Legoman Biffo recordings and detailed with full bufferbeam pipework and subtle weathering as most DRS locomotives are generally quite clean. The vast majority of the locos seen on The Sidings are DRS owned but visits from Colas, West Coast, GB Railfreight and Network Rail motive power also occur.

ABOVE: The inspiration for the layout, York Parcels Sidings, is often used to stable DRS locos engaged on engineering duties or Railhead Treatment Trains. Perhaps this is where 20303 *Max Joule 1958-1999* and 37602 are off to as the duo depart the stabling point.

ABOVE LEFT AND ABOVE RIGHT: Two views of the principal scenic details on the layout, showing the largely scratchbuilt GSM-R radio mast and associated building as well as the contractors at work on the relay cabinets. Visible in the foreground is one of the point heaters. Details such as this help to bring a layout to life, especially if they are scratchbuilt or modified propriety items to give an individual touch.

Stabling points

ABOVE: Network Rail's 31233 keeps 57304 *Pride of Cheshire* company as the pair pose in front of the Rawie friction bufferstops. These are completely scratchbuilt from plastic strip and sheet, predating the Accurascale models.

LEFT: Both the layout and fiddle yard are designed to accommodate two vehicle formations, meaning that more than single locos can be operated, creating further interest. In this view, Network Rail's track recording DMU 950001 is laying over between legs of its diagram, this being a Bachmann model modified with the PH Designs etches.

RIGHT: The inspiration for The Sidings is provided by 37419 *Driver Tony Kay* at rest in York Parcels Sidings on July 16, 2023. While the trackplan has been transplanted to the layout, the background has not, this largely consisting of York Rail Operating Centre, just out of view to the left.
Steven Brykajlo

18 www.keymodelworld.com

Stabling points

Bufferstop variations

Pretty much every depot layout needs bufferstops in some quantity or other. Terry Bendall **builds a typical BR pattern with the aid of a useful detailing etch while various types are illustrated.**

Scenic work and attention to small details are the things that turn a model railway layout into a model of the railway. In order to do this effectively, research is often needed, and while it takes a bit of time, it is not difficult to do and can be quite absorbing as an activity anyway.

For the modeller of the current railway scene, research can be quite easy - just go out and look at what is there and take pictures. For anything in the past, be it 10, 20, or 50 years ago, it is necessary to look at books or use the vast range of information that is available on the internet. Although many pictures may be focussed on a locomotive or train, looking around the edges of the picture will often reveal details of such things as buildings, signals, bridges, and other infrastructure items. There are also plenty of sources of information about these sorts of things in their own right.

ABOVE: The two stabling roads known as York Parcels Sidings feature a basic version of the Rawie bufferstop without the coupling pocket, as seen on June 23, 2014. The Accurascale model is all but identical to this, while both have extended track sections provided behind to allow for push-back, albeit without fiction pads. Simon Bendall

ABOVE: During 2014, a new servicing area for Railhead Treatment Trains was constructed in part of Tonbridge West Yard, this seeing new sidings laid alongside existing ones that were refurbished. As a result, there is quite a contrast between the two, most obviously in the bufferstop design. Nearest the camera on December 12 that year is one of the older BR stops with, surprisingly, only one crossbeam made out of rail. Beyond are two newly installed Rawie bufferstops with much more substantial construction. The two new lines also employ flat bottom track on concrete sleepers right to their end while the original sidings retain a short length of bullhead rail on wooden sleepers. Beneath the crossing, this transitions to flat bottom rail on wooden sleepers for the rest of the old sidings. Mixing of bufferstops at depots has been common over the years. Simon Bendall

The humble bufferstop is a case in point as while it is simplicity itself to install a ready-made plastic version from the likes of Hornby or Peco, there was considerable variation in the appearance of such items. Some railway companies had particularly distinctive designs and as bufferstops had long lives, these lasted well into the diesel era so picking the right style can help set the geographical area in which your depot is set. In 4mm scale, Lanarkshire Models and Supplies offers by far the most comprehensive range available with 28 different styles currently listed.

British Rail naturally adopted its own standard designs, which evolved over the years, and these are still found today, frequently mixed together. There were also various hydraulic designs, although these tended to be more for station use, while an array of new styles has appeared in more recent decades, many supplied

ABOVE: Of Accurascale's Rawie bufferstop models, this is the most advanced with two working red LED lights when wired up to a 12 volt supply. The coupling box attachment, in this case configured for a Scharfenberg coupling, can be seen in the centre. Rawie incorporates such a feature where required as the coupling on modern multiple units would normally be the first thing to hit a bufferstop.

ABOVE: Derived from an LMS design, this bufferstop style was one of BR's favoured types and is available in 4mm from Lanarkshire Models and Supplies. Seen at Carlisle Kingmoor on July 16, 2011. Simon Bendall

ABOVE: Of London & North Western Railway design, this bufferstop still retained its original wooden top at Crewe Gresty Bridge on July 10, 2010. Lanarkshire offers the style with replacement rail crossbeam. Simon Bendall

Modelling BR: Diesel Depots 19

Stabling points

by Rawie. With a history dating back 150 years, the company is now the world-leader in bufferstop technology, and its products feature widely on the UK system, including at modern maintenance depots.

Accurascale is currently the only supplier of Rawie bufferstops in 4mm scale, its products being for OO gauge only. Three different types are available, encompassing a basic version, one with a coupling box attachment and the third with functioning LED buffer lights. In all cases, they are supplied with friction pads, these going on extended rail lengths behind the bufferstop to arrest its travel in the event of a collision.

Building a bufferstop

ABOVE: The etch containing the gusset plates and cutting templates as supplied by PH Designs.

RIGHT: Nine lengths of Code 75 bullhead rail, which is not supplied with the etch, need to be cut to length and filed to shape, this giving the six legs and three crossbeams.

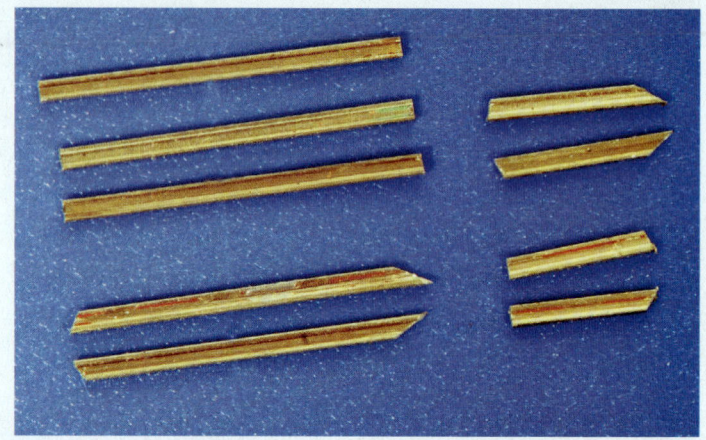

An etch for one of the most common BR styles of bufferstop is available from PH Designs (www.phd-design-etchings.co.uk), this providing gusset plates in etched brass that need to be combined with lengths of rail cut to length, the etch incorporating a template to achieve this.

To construct the bufferstop, a punch is required to first push out the half-etched rivets in the gusset plates while Code 75 bullhead rail is also needed. The rail is cut to the requisite lengths and the ends profiled using the template as a guide. These are then soldered up using the gusset plates at the joints. It is important to check that both sides of the bufferstop are an exact match with each other in terms of leg angles as otherwise it will not be square.

It is best to assemble the bufferstop on a separate short length of track, threading the two sides onto the sleeper bases. This saves having to assemble the bufferstop in-situ on a baseboard and, as it is entirely metal, makes it easier to insulate it from the running rails. Once the two sides are in place, the three lengths of rail that make up the face of the bufferstop can be soldered across between them and small details such as the L-shaped mounting brackets and bolt strengthening plates added. Colours tend to be black, red, or white, sometimes with a different colour of crossbeam.

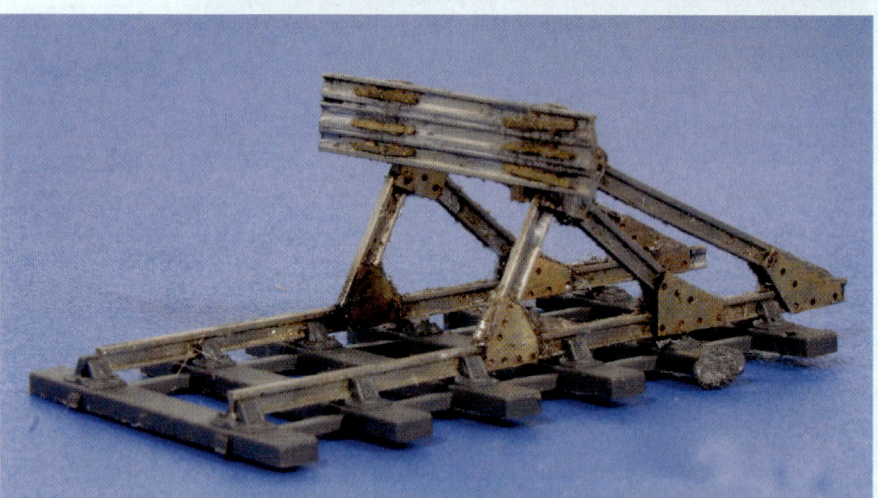

ABOVE: With the two sides threaded onto the sleeper base, the rails forming the crossbeam can be soldered across and the small bolt strengthening plates added to the front.

ABOVE: One side of the bufferstop is shown assembled and soldered to a short length of rail, with the four gusset plates also in place.

ABOVE: From the rear, the L-shaped mounting brackets behind the crossbeam can be seen, Once assembled, the flux and solder can be cleaned off and the bufferstop painted.

WEST HILL WAGON WORKS
Model Railway Detailed Accessories • Hunt Magnetic Couplings

Diesel Fuelling Point **Locomotive Stands**

15 Ton Vehicle Lifting Jacks **Class 37 Power Unit** **Depot Interior Kits**

& Much More!

Special Offer For Hornby Magazine/Key Publishing Readers!
Get 10% Discount Using Code: **HornbyMagazine10** At Checkout
Checkout Over **600** Products For Your Model Railway Online At
www.westhillwagonworks.co.uk

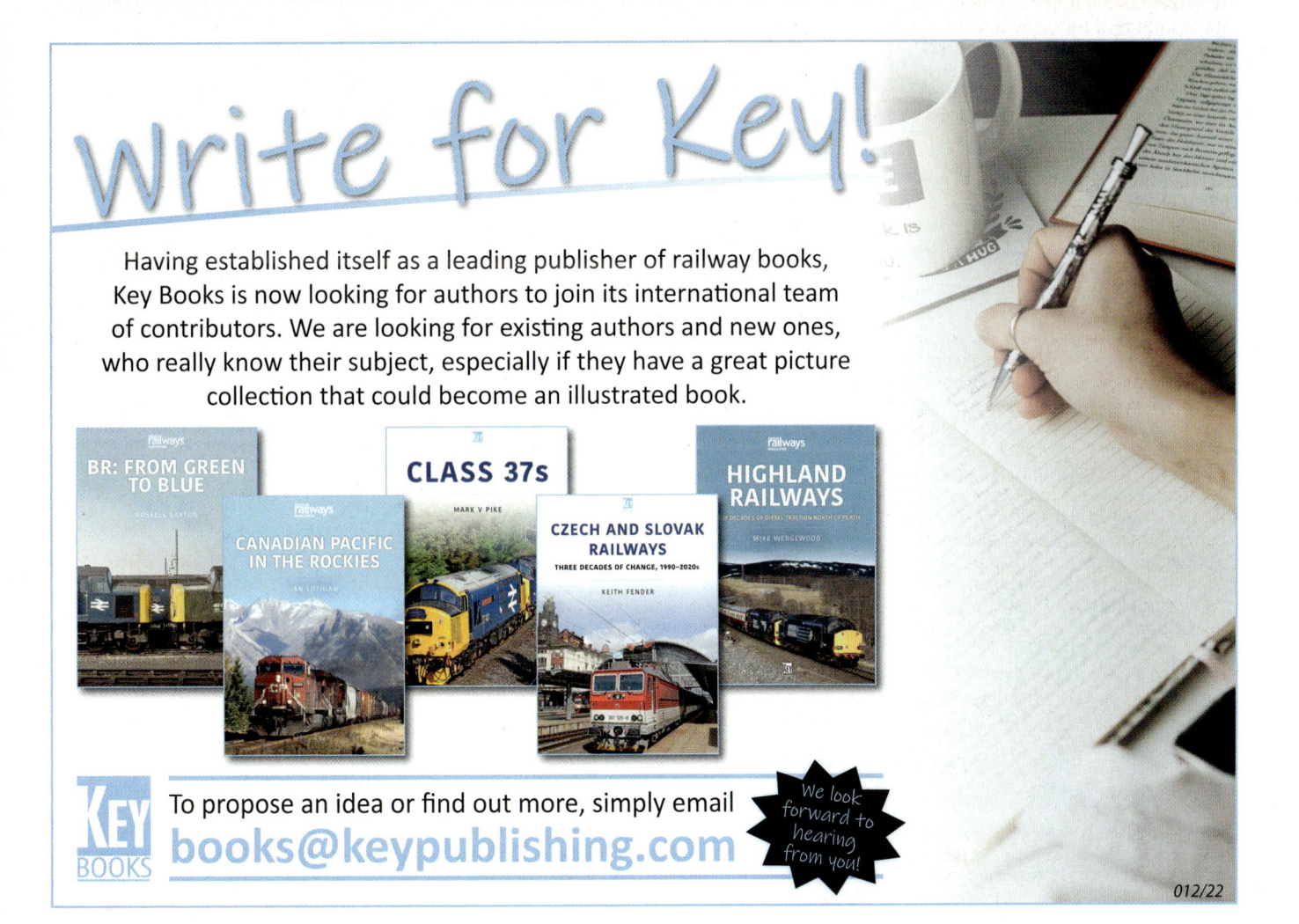

Write for Key!

Having established itself as a leading publisher of railway books, Key Books is now looking for authors to join its international team of contributors. We are looking for existing authors and new ones, who really know their subject, especially if they have a great picture collection that could become an illustrated book.

BR: FROM GREEN TO BLUE
CANADIAN PACIFIC IN THE ROCKIES
CLASS 37s — MARK V PIKE
CZECH AND SLOVAK RAILWAYS — THREE DECADES OF CHANGE, 1990-2020s — KEITH FENDER
HIGHLAND RAILWAYS

KEY BOOKS

To propose an idea or find out more, simply email
books@keypublishing.com

We look forward to hearing from you!

012/22

Loco inspection points

Moving up a level from stabling points, loco inspection points, or servicing depots as they were sometimes also known, could carry out fuelling and light servicing activities in addition to providing stabling. Typical of the facilities favoured by modellers, **Simon Bendall** looks at their characteristics.

Falling in the category between simple stabling points and well equipped traction maintenance depots were the group of facilities known as locomotive inspection points (LIP) or servicing depots. Although somewhat diverse in nature, these invariably had fuelling facilities and the ability to carry out the more minor exam work. An inspection pit and limited covered accommodation, often enough for just one or two locos, was typically provided alongside staff amenities.

It is this type of depot that often inspires many smaller sized layouts, being the sort of facility that can be squeezed onto a short baseboard of 4ft or less. Add in a couple of stabling sidings and you have a layout with sufficient 'play value' to be entertaining. Typically, a LIP would not have the ability to carry out more heavy duty repairs, such as any type of loco or component lifting, so any traction requiring such repairs would be forwarded onto a TMD.

Depending on the age and region of the depot, the fuelling facilities could either be found inside the shed building or located externally, the former option allowing an even smaller layout to be created and still be realistic. Fuel storage tanks would be required with either road or rail delivery. The former would be more common in later decades, but local access could force a rail delivery for extra interest.

For example, the fuelling point at Ipswich still received its fuel, or traction gas oil to be correct, by rail right up until closure in July 2022, there being no road access. During the 2000s, this was sourced from the refinery at Fawley, near Southampton, and delivered in Esso-owned two-axle TTA tankers by EWS and then DB. However, when this service was withdrawn in March 2015, Freightliner was forced to introduce a new arrangement.

This saw a Freightliner Class 66, or occasionally a Class 70 when they still worked regularly in East Anglia, trip a short rake of tankers all the way from Lindsey refinery in North Lincolnshire to Ipswich. The tankers employed varied over the years, the initial period of operation and later years seeing modern TDA and TEA bogie tanks utilised, the latter being produced in both N gauge and OO gauge by Revolution Trains. Normally, one, two or three bogie tanks were sufficient for the needs of the fuelling point, resulting in a bizarre but highly modellable short train. For a time in the late 2010s, VTG-owned TTAs still in the obsolete BP green and yellow scheme were deployed, typically loading to between two and six wagons, or sometimes with a mix of TTA and TDA/TEA. Even in today's world of long bulk trains, there is still the occasional oddity to be found!

ABOVE: Constructed during 1994, the small depot at Didcot brought fuelling and servicing facilities to the Oxfordshire yard in order to support the introduction of power station coal workings from Avonmouth Docks. Previously, these workings had originated from collieries in the Midlands, allowing locos to be serviced at Toton, but with the switch to imported coal, alternative arrangements were required. By August 25, 2000, the depot was in EWS ownership as Mainline Freight-liveried 60011 is refuelled. Simon Bendall Collection

Loco inspection points

LEFT: A closer look at the servicing shed at Didcot on July 15, 1995, finds 37051 lurking inside, while the fuel pump is equipped with a rudimentary shelter. Two tall but narrow diameter fuel storage tanks are provided down the side of the building, these being replenished by road tanker. Other details include long-handled brushes and a blue container by the shed door lettered 'Diluted Exmover Loco Wash', this being the legendary chemical detergent used for cleaning rolling stock, and which would strip the paint as well as the dirt if applied too concentrated for too long! *Simon Bendall Collection*

ABOVE: The servicing and fuelling point at Westbury was provided with two covered shelters, each having an inspection pit below, as locos were outbased here for the Mendips aggregates traffic. These sheds were originally both open ended but the early 1980s saw one have roller shutter doors added, giving it a squared off appearance compared to the original peaked roof. The revised look is seen on June 29, 1991, as 56052 stands in the second, unmodified shelter behind. Colas still uses Westbury for maintenance today but with a modern shed building built as a replacement. *Simon Bendall Collection*

ABOVE LEFT AND ABOVE RIGHT: A small servicing and fuelling depot was provided at Severn Tunnel Junction, given the considerable number of locos that were normally to be found around the marshalling yard. However, the stabling roads alongside the depot building were rather deserted on February 12, 1987, as closure loomed with just 37697 and 37227 awaiting their next duty. The short spur road could accommodate up to three Class 08s, albeit buffered up and a snug fit, while a single main line loco could also occupy the line. Seen through the open doors of the shed is 47237 while the two horizontal fuel storage tanks can just be glimpsed. The tanker road for replenishing these was immediately adjacent as was the small water tower. Even for a small building, a considerable amount of equipment and clutter can be seen, including a battery charger, four-wheel sack truck and all important bicycle for a fitter! *Simon Bendall Collection*

Modelling BR: Diesel Depots

Loco inspection points

ABOVE: The stabling point alongside Ipswich station was a cut above many others, having a fuelling point and inspection pit but no covered accommodation. As Felixstowe grew into the UK's most important intermodal facility, Ipswich was increasingly used by traction employed on the container traffic. This reached its natural conclusion upon privatisation with Freightliner becoming the primary user of the stabling point and maintenance facilities. With traction changes taking place in the nearby yard, enthusiasts could observe a regular flow of diesel and electric traction working on and off the sidings. However, come the early 2020s, Freightliner had outgrown the yard, opting to build a new depot with greatly expanded facilities in the under-utilised yard, this being commissioned in July 2022. As a result, the stabling point is now largely used by Greater Anglia and for weekend stabling of Freightliner Class 90s. On October 8, 2020, 66550 and 66557 are prominent with 66413, 66529 and a further Class 66/5 also present as are 'Flirts' 755416 and 755330. Just visible beneath the trees between the two Class 66s are the TEAs used on the Linsey fuel working, while to the right of the picture and partly obscured by the bush is KFA container flat TIPH93366. This carried two blue-painted 20ft containers and was used to deliver parts and consumables to the maintenance area due to the lack of road access. Jim Ramsay

ABOVE: An early 1990s view finds 08414 resting behind the fuelling point at Ipswich and sitting over the inspection pit. The two short spurs pointing in opposite directions maximised the space available in this cramped area with Shell-branded TTA SUKO65533 on the opposing line. Again, the diverse collection of clutter on show is highly modellable, complete with a scaffolding tower and portable building. Simon Bendall Collection

ABOVE: On the same day as 08414, classmate 08767 was stabled atop the TTAs with SUKO65741 for company. The fuel storage tanks can be seen behind the shunter. Although much of the stabling point was electrified in the mid-1980s when the Great Eastern Main Line was done, the fuelling and maintenance roads were not, meaning any AC electric requiring attention over the pit had to be shunted into place. Simon Bendall Collection

Loco inspection points

LEFT: The small servicing depot at King's Lynn followed conventional 1960s Eastern Region construction with extensive use of glazing in the sides and an inspection pit. The fuelling points were sited outside though, with other typical features including the fuel storage tank and water tower. The depot looked after the needs of the shunters assigned to work the yard, harbour, and station as well as diesel traction arriving on passenger and freight services. On May 16, 1986, 08713 was in residence. *Simon Bendall Collection*

RIGHT: Peterborough LIP employed considerably less glazing but had the fuelling facilities installed inside the single road shed, rather than opting for an external fuel point. Although it survived in use into EWS ownership, the decline of traffic in the yards at Peterborough in the early 2000s together with the rebirth of March Whitemoor Yard as the area's infrastructure hub ensured the depot's closure. On June 15, 2017, 66115 was stabled alongside, still retaining its obsolete EWS branding. A maintenance facility still exists in Peterborough today, GB Railfreight having established a modern depot about half a mile away. *Craig Adamson*

LEFT: One of the earliest releases in Bachmann's range of Scenecraft resin buildings in 4mm scale was a recreation of Peterborough LIP, this being a faithful representation and also nicely finished. Unsurprisingly, it proved to be extremely popular and has been re-run on further occasions as a result. Perfectly sized for a small layout, one is seen installed on Alex Carpenter's Meadow Lane with 47238 *Bescot Yard* keeping company with a soon to be withdrawn Class 45/1. *Alex Carpenter*

Modelling BR: Diesel Depots

Loco inspection points

An unusual viewpoint

Now two decades old, Villier Street remains an interesting exercise in building a stabling point, its triangular baseboard being designed to be viewed end on. Originally built by Tony Woof, it subsequently passed to Ian Manderson, who presents a selection of views of the layout.

Villier Street was originally built for the 2003 small layout competition of the Diesel & Electric Modellers United (DEMU) society, which it duly won. Measuring six feet long, including the sector plate fiddle yard, it is one foot, six inches across at the widest point of the scenic section, with the track built to EM gauge.

Having decided on the unusual triangular shape and view point, a friend with theatrical experience was consulted who explained about employing scenic sets to control the viewing angles and using forced perspective. This called for tall sides and an inner end to frame the layout, giving it a particularly dingy and urban feel and of being squeezed into the space that was available. Three lines radiate out from the sector plate with two points then featuring on the layout, giving a total of five roads by the time the bufferstops are reached.

By being deliberately generic with the scenery, it enables the layout to portray almost any region during the 1970s, allowing the locos that are present to set the era and location. For example, BRCW Type 2s and a Class 17 'Clayton' will instantly create a Scottish flavour while the same is true with Western Region hydraulics, Class 31s on the Eastern and so on. Equally, the locos can be with pre-TOPS identities or following renumbering, creating further modelling options. Adding the odd wagon, brake van or snowplough along with a shunter or two creates further operating potential and ensures that, despite its small size, the layout is never boring.

ABOVE: A typical London Midland scene in the mid-1970s as 25109 brings in fuel tanks to replenish the fuel storage tanks that are just out of view to the right. The Class 47 still in two-tone green further helps set the period, while adding plenty of height using the retaining walls and buildings on top frames the scene. *Ian Manderson*

RIGHT: The Midlands and northwest in the corporate era are again recalled as 40118 and 25242 rest on the fuelling point. This is the trusty Knightwing plastic kit with a few minor alterations, while the spear fencing is from Ratio. Considered use of scenic material around the fence and on top of the retaining walls further contributes to the look of urban decay along with adding some colour. *Ian Manderson*

Loco inspection points

ABOVE: Using models of certain loco classes will instantly set the region of the layout, 'Hymeks' 7018 and 7076 bringing an unmistakable Western look to proceedings alongside a Class 25. The bridge girders are from Ratio while the use of ash-like ballast is a further scenic touch as BR-era depots were rarely properly ballasted. Ian Manderson

ABOVE: A quick swap of locos moves Villier Street to Scotland as a trio of Type 2s of Classes 25, 26 and 27 keep a Class 06 and Class 08 company. While the layout may only be small in size, the trick of widening the perspective ensures it does not look crowded, even with five locos on show. Ian Manderson

Modelling BR: Diesel Depots   **27**

Diesel depot development

Different regions adopted different designs of shed building to suit their needs, Simon Bendall sets out these basic principles before taking a pictorial look at a variety of examples.

When the Modernisation Plan was published in 1955, it set out a scheme to completely replace the prevailing steam traction with an entirely new locomotive fleet consisting of both diesel and electric traction. However, this simple aim masked the sea change in maintenance that would be necessary to allow the much smaller fleet to achieve the utilisation levels envisaged.

Early diesel traction up to this point had been maintained alongside their steam counterparts, sharing the same dusty, dirty steam sheds with little, if any, segregation. This had already confirmed that diesels did not like such conditions, where soot and dust was pulled into ventilation grilles, clogging up the internals and contributing to poor reliability. If the new order were to succeed, it was clear that it would need its own dedicated maintenance facilities while the protracted transition from steam took place. Other issues included a lack of staff with any knowledge of how to maintain electrical systems and no proper fuelling facilities, resulting in some lash-ups that were at best risky if not outright dangerous.

Some initial consideration was given to adapting steam sheds on the Eastern, London Midland and Western regions but this was largely ruled out on cost and suitably grounds, the needs of the two types varying too widely. While it did happen, this was largely on secondary routes with new

ABOVE: Two Class 50s, both in Network SouthEast livery, stand inside the fuelling and servicing shed at Old Oak Common in January 1990, the one in the centre being 50024 *Vanguard*. When the depot was converted from steam to diesel, this building was the most significant addition to the previous Great Western-built structures.
Simon Bendall Collection

build instead preferred for the busiest lines. For all the plans of the British Transport Commission, it lacked experience in the operation of diesels so fact finding missions were undertaken to the United States, where the new order had already been widely operating for a decade. Armed with some insight from the US, each region was largely left to go its own way with developing their depots in the absence of instructions from on high, resulting in a divergence of ideas as the 1960s began.

Maintenance vs servicing

Both the Eastern and Western regions adopted the philosophy that maintenance and servicing of diesel locos were two different activities and, as a result, the functions were to be kept separate. This resulted in major depots on these two regions typically having two sheds, the servicing shed for fuelling, topping up of other fluids and consumables, and basic checks to A and B exam level. If anything more involved was required, the loco would be directed to the maintenance shed for attention. The other four regions went the opposite way, taking the view that it was all maintenance in some form or another and could be done under one roof, with the fuelling done outside.

With the Eastern Region being the first to receive the new diesel classes in large quantities for workings out of Liverpool Street and King's Cross, the initial purpose-built diesel depots duly appeared on the two routes out of London and spread from there. The first large maintenance depots to be completed were at Stratford and Finsbury Park, the region eventually building ten maintenance depots and 24 servicing depots.

The region's philosophy on maintenance depot design was to have dead end bays at each end of the shed and a central area for stores, work areas and other amenities. However, this was not shared by the other regions, which preferred at least some double-ended roads to give optimum throughput of locos and prevent anything becoming stuck on a dead end line.

On some regions, there was a reluctance to invest in heavy lifting equipment at depots because it greatly increased the costs of construction at a time when budgets were being squeezed. The argument against was that each region had at least one

Diesel depot development

major workshop to call its own, so any repairs requiring component lifts could be done there.

Other regions
On the London Midland Region, the first diesel depot to be established was at Devons Road, Bow, this being a LMR shed even though it was in East London. The depot was envisaged to be a guinea pig for the ideas brought over from America mixed in with a few homegrown ones as well. This was an extensively converted single-ended steam shed with half of it turned over to maintenance, complete with pits and elevated walkways, which was segregated from the rest of the depot, this being used for stabling. It was experience of operating this depot that put the LMR off dead-end maintenance roads for good, with through roads specified in the future whenever possible.

Elsewhere, the Southern Region had only a small diesel fleet to contend with and this was largely dealt with by modifying Stewarts Lane and constructing a new depot at Eastleigh. For a time, the Class 33s shared shed space with steam at Hither Green, leading to all the inevitable problems of contamination, this not being properly resolved until steam was withdrawn.

It was in Scotland were the practice of converting steam sheds for diesel and DMU use was most common as, while the results were often unsatisfactory, it was cheaper than building new depots. Even Eastfield was originally a converted steam shed before it was completely rebuilt at the end of the 1960s. The North Eastern Region often followed the same practice as north of the border, adapting the likes of Bradford Hammerton Street for example.

However, at both Thornaby and Gateshead, rebuilding work was already in progress when the Modernisation Plan was

ABOVE: Shirebrook was one of the servicing depots constructed by the Eastern Region, the two-road single-ended shed following established practice by featuring lots of glass. The first two Class 56s to be delivered new in BR large logo, 56084 and 56085, repose outside the depot on February 21, 1981, having been delivered the previous autumn. Simon Bendall Collection

ABOVE: The opening of March depot in 1963 ensured that steam was gone from former Great Eastern metals by the end of that year. 25 years later, Railfreight Distribution's 47377 was stabled on depot having worked over from Whitemoor Yard. However, the declining fortunes of the marshalling yard also affected the depot, and it closed in 1992 after the withdrawal of the Speedlink wagonload network decimated what freight remained in the area. Simon Bendall Collection

Modelling BR: Diesel Depots 29

Diesel depot development

ABOVE: The maintenance depot at Tinsley was the culmination of Eastern Region practice regarding loco repair facilities when it was completed in 1964. The building was laid out in the now established manner with dead-end repairs bays at both ends of the shed and a central stores and workshops. New features included a locomotive wash plant, which was now deemed essential equipment rather than a desirable feature. The servicing depot was located at a lower level alongside the yard, to which fuel was pumped from the maintenance shed. The south end of the depot is seen on August 14, 1994, but four years later it would be closed. *Simon Bendall Collection*

announced. As a result, both schemes were adapted part way through to make the shed suitable for diesel conversion the following decade. The result in both cases was a compromise with track layouts not optimised to diesels and main buildings with low roofs. However, the work was cheaper than new build, something that was becoming rather clear at board level as the cost of a country-wide investment plan hit home.

For the London Midland Region, the completion of Toton in 1965 gave it a showpiece to rival the best of the Eastern and Western regions, it being publicised as the largest diesel depot in Western Europe on completion. Its 15 roads at the north end of the depot building were split between servicing, mid-level maintenance and heavy repairs with only five exiting from the south end.

On the Western
Laira was the first of the new Western Region diesel depots to be completed, it being a lavish affair with several unique design traits in the appearance of the buildings. However, it was so expensive that a tight reign was kept on the depots that followed, such as Canton and Landore,

ABOVE: Still in BR blue, 37096 is seen stabled outside the south end of Tinsley in June 1989. A glimpse into the depot behind shows the short nature of the repair bays with the dividing wall for the centre stores area visible. As with virtually all of its depots, extensive use of glass was favoured, which is a design trait that can instantly make an Eastern Region depot stand out on a layout. *Simon Bendall Collection*

Diesel depot development

with specifications laid out in great detail. Disputes would ensue between upper management and dept managers over the provision of equipment that one party felt was needed and the other did not.

Bristol Bath Road was partly spared such concerns as it re-used steam-era buildings that had been built in the 1930s, these forming the heavy repair and maintenance sheds. This just left the servicing shed to be constructed near to Temple Meads, complete with the requisite fuelling facilities. Old Oak Common similarly saw a mix of conversion and new build with the Factory retained for heavy repairs, while the four roundhouses were all demolished to make way for the new servicing shed, leaving one of the turntables behind. When the West London depot was re-commissioned in 1965, it marked the completion of the Western's diesel depot network and the end of steam on the Great Western.

ABOVE: Toton was the crown jewel for the London Midland Region on completion in 1965, when it served the considerable needs of the surrounding coalfields and other heavy industries. That it still serves as DB Cargo's principal UK depot today is a testament to how well designed it was and it is still relatively unchanged, except for an extension to accommodate heavy lifting equipment. Around 1970, Class 25 5267 heads a line-up of typical LMR motive power. Simon Bendall Collection

LEFT: A near spotless 47621 *Royal County of Berkshire* is seen at Tyseley in 1986 with one of the depot's resident Class 08s. Although best known as a DMU depot, main line locos could be found here in BR days. The mix of roller shutter and concertina depot doors is notable as is the style of the roof, which exhibits more design flair that usual for a depot. Simon Bendall Collection

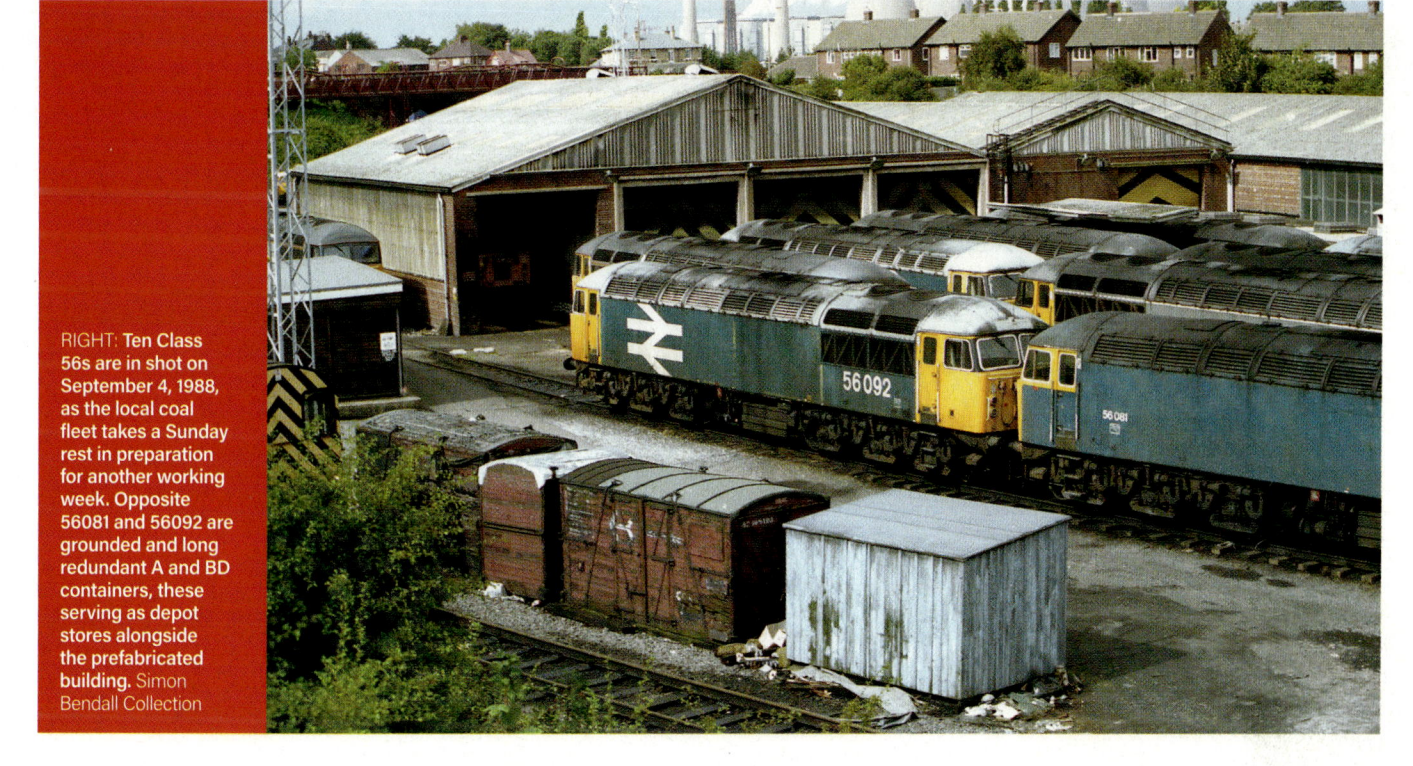

RIGHT: Ten Class 56s are in shot on September 4, 1988, as the local coal fleet takes a Sunday rest in preparation for another working week. Opposite 56081 and 56092 are grounded and long redundant A and BD containers, these serving as depot stores alongside the prefabricated building. Simon Bendall Collection

Modelling BR: Diesel Depots 31

Diesel depot development

ABOVE: Diesel loco maintenance on the Southern Region was traditionally divided between Eastleigh, Stewarts Lane, and Hither Green during the British Rail era. Having worked in from the Western Region, 56001 *Whatley* utilises the fuelling point at Hither Green. Under EWS ownership, this was later enclosed as the depot was enhanced following privatisation and the loco side of Stewarts Lane closed. Simon Bendall Collection

BELOW: An equally unique depot dealing in underground stock is the Waterloo & City line facility beneath the London terminus. Seen in the gloom on January 17, 1980, is driving motor S60. The vehicles would normally only come to the surface for major works attention. Simon Bendall Collection

ABOVE: Heading across the Solent to the Isle of Wight, the maintenance depot at Ryde is illustrated on July 27, 1984, while services were still in the hands of the Class 485 and Class 486 former London Underground 'standard' stock. The depot was an amalgamation of the former steam shed and new build, and little has changed in 2023. Simon Bendall Collection

Diesel depot development

ABOVE: **In Scotland, the new diesel fleet had to adapt to using steam era facilities. Such was the case at Oban on July 7, 1965, as two BRCW Type 2s (later Class 27) stand by the coaling facilities while a third member of the class shunts the yard. The former loco depot is the building to the left of shot. Prominent at the front of the picture is independent snowplough DB965200 in the original plain black livery.** Simon Bendall Collection

ABOVE: **The Scottish Region considered that many steam sheds were adaptable for diesel use, not least because it saved money on new construction. Inverness was one such location, although by the time 47460 and 37261** *Caithness* **were pictured outside in May 1987, more modern facilities had been built alongside.** Simon Bendall Collection

Modelling BR: Diesel Depots 33

Diesel depot development

LEFT: Another Scottish steam shed turned over to maintaining diesel traction during the 1960s was Grangemouth, this lasting longer than most thanks to its proximity to the nearby docks and refineries. A basic fuelling point was installed to serve one road of the running shed, and this is seen on September 28, 1987, with 20198 taking centre stage alongside a Class 47. The split-headcode Class 37 is occupying the single road maintenance shed, this being equipped with a roller shutter door, unlike the rest of the shed which was open to the elements. Simon Bendall Collection

RIGHT: Nowadays, the depot at Fort William owes its continuing existence to West Coast's 'Jacobite' steam operation between Fort William and Mallaig, all other uses of the facility having come to an end. Back in BR days though, it played host to ScotRail stock alongside the steam service as well as freight as OTA timber wagons were loaded from a siding. Illustrating much of this diversity, 37407 *Loch Long* and 37422 were on shed on September 28, 1988, with an unidentified Class 20. The depot buildings have always been a bit of a mash-up, giving it a shanty-town appearance. Simon Bendall Collection

ABOVE: Coming back south to the Western Region, the conversion of Old Oak Common to maintain diesel traction was completed in 1965, the Great Western Railway-built Factory becoming a heavy repair shop. Some 21 years later in September 1986, a gleaming 47515 stands outside the depot having just ben repainted in InterCity Executive colours. The depot staff were a dab hand with a paintbrush during the 1980s and 1990s, outshopping several celebrities as well as numerous locos in Intercity, Network SouthEast, Rail Express Systems and Civil Engineers 'Dutch'. Simon Bendall Collection

Diesel depot development

ABOVE: The servicing shed at Old Oak Common is seen from the turntable end on November 15, 2008. While end views are common in pictures, the depot sides were less often pictured so this shot reveals plenty of useful details. The skips for scrap metal clearly need emptying as well! Bachmann has previously released a depot building heavily influenced by this structure, the ends and roof being particularly good, although the sides were rather freelance and the worse for it. *Simon Bendall*

LEFT: A view across Bristol Bath Road on March 21, 1978, is dominated by the heavy repair shop, this building dating from the 1930s but deemed suitable for conversion to diesel use thanks to its high roof. With the servicing shed and Temple Meads off to the left, 50040 and 50042 dominate the line-up with 45065 behind. The odd oil drum would appear to be surplus! *Simon Bendall Collection*

RIGHT: Viewed from the platforms at Temple Meads, the front of the servicing shed at Bristol Bath Road is seen on August 7, 1990, with the taller heavy repair shop of the previous image in the background. On shed are 56031 *Merehead*, 47283 *Jonnie walker* and 50008 *Thunderer* with a rubbed down and unidentified HST power car part way through a repaint into InterCity Swallow. Like its West London rival, Bath Road often splashed the paint about, mostly on InterCity traction. *Simon Bendall Collection*

Modelling BR: Diesel Depots 35

Diesel depot development

ABOVE AND LEFT: Moving south west, Exeter was the next maintenance location to be encountered. The walls of the former steam shed still stand in the panoramic shot taken on June 22, 1997, with two Class 37s, Class 117 and 121 DMUs and unique tamper DR75101 present. These walls have been partly re-used to support a roof over the fuelling point while a small servicing depot is further back. The latter is better seen on June 21, 1989, with 50018 *Resolution* present, locos on the Waterloo-Exeter circuit often visiting between turns. Simon Bendall Collection

RIGHT: Class 50 pioneer D400 was still an interloper as far a diesel hydraulic fans were concerned when recorded at Laira in December 1973, 14 months after arriving on the region to herald the arrival of the new order. The modernistic design of the depot, completed just over a decade earlier, was certainly eye-catching but it was also expensive, causing Western Region officials to take a much tighter control of the purse strings for future facilities. Simon Bendall Collection

36 www.keymodelworld.com

Diesel depot development

ABOVE: The Western agreed with the Eastern that the best way to care for diesels was to have separate servicing and maintenance buildings. The heavy repair shop is seen at Laira on January 11, 1992, this following the same principle of having dead end roads and raised walkways. On this occasion, 50007 *Sir Edward Elgar* and 37673 were against the stops with two HST power cars and two Class 37s blocking them in, illustrating the main problem with this shed layout. Simon Bendall Collection

ABOVE: During their ill-fated introduction on the Cornish branches, 'Skipper' 142023 rests outside the wagon maintenance depot at St Blazey on August 30, 1987. With the roundhouse very restricted in terms of space and access, the wagon building was increasingly used for other stock as well, taking on this role fully under EWS and now DB Cargo. The OOV clay hoods alongside only had another six months left in traffic. Simon Bendall Collection

LEFT: Trainload Metals-liveried 56044 *Cardiff Canton* was at home in March 1992 as it rests outside the wheel lathe building at its namesake. Built around 1988, this was a large building by the standards of some lathes as it also contained an overhead gantry crane. The then modern cladding rather stood out amidst the rest of the depot as well. Simon Bendall Collection

Modelling BR: Diesel Depots

Diesel depot development

With the demise of Yorkshire coal traffic, Knottingley has lost its purpose in recent years, 2023 just about seeing the depot still open for fuelling and servicing of DB locos engaged on biomass traffic and as a host while Mk.2f coaches belonging to Riviera Trains are modified with controlled emission tanks. Closure will inevitably come like it has for so many DB depots, but a celebratory line-up of motive power was staged on February 29, 2020, with, from left, 67005 *Queen's Messenger*, 66099, 66051 *Maritime Intermodal Four*, 66107 and 66074. Adrian Nicholls

Freightliner's vehicle maintenance facility (VMF) at Basford Hall is seen shortly after completion on November 11, 2016. The depot had hosted a naming ceremony for Remembrance Day earlier when 66418 was named *Patriot* in honour of the 20,000 railwaymen that lost their lives in the First World War. Following this, it was posed with 66614 *Poppy 1916-2016* and a British Army MAN HX60 general utility truck from the Mercian Regiment for an all green line-up. Below the Freightliner sign, solar panels are installed to contribute to the depot's power requirements. Simon Bendall

Diesel depot development

ABOVE: **The Leeds Midland Road depot of Freightliner is seen on July 24, 2010, seven years after it opened. By this date, an overhead gantry crane had been added, which would soon be enclosed in its own building. The depot also carried out maintenance on the company's wagon fleet with coal hoppers stabled alongside the shed and bogies frames piled up by the fence. This has now rather reduced following the end of Freightliner's power station coal traffic.** Simon Bendall Collection

BELOW: **One of the most recent depots to see investment is Leicester, where a new maintenance shed has been constructed ahead of the arrival of the new Class 99 electric hybrid locos. This takes centre stage in this July 3, 2023, view with the locos on shed being 69008, 69007, 37003, 67027, 56081, 56103, 37905, 47727, 56301 and 47749. The former BR depot is to the right of the shed, this having seen some extensions since passing to UK Rail Leasing control while the fuelling point was also upgraded a few years ago to fuel CrossCountry Class 170s.** Jim Ramsey

Modelling BR: Diesel Depots **39**

Diesel depot development

ABOVE: An overview of the front of DRS' Crewe Gresty Bridge depot on March 11, 2014, with 20312 most prominent. This shows the depot in its fully modernised form with the extension on the servicing shed, new fuelling shelter, and stores building further back, all finished in a rather fetching blue and green. *Simon Bendall*

LEFT, BELOW LEFT AND BELOW RIGHT: The method of extending the existing brick-built depot at Gresty Bridge is shown in these three photos, DRS originally re-cladding the depot frontage as seen in July 2008. When the depot was extended, the previous frontage was retained and became the new internal wall. Viewed from the rear in October 2012, the new height and width compared to the old building can be seen. This offers some interesting modelling potential by showing how a steam era structure could be modernised to form a modern depot, rather than just using a modern, fairly soulless steel construction. *Simon Bendall*

Diesel depot development

ABOVE: The final three photos take a look at carriage sheds, a category that you do not often see modelled despite them allowing locos and stock to be portrayed together in a depot environment. Still used by South Western Railway today, 47825 and its Mk.2 set stand in Bournemouth depot on May 7, 1989. The formation would later work empty to Poole to form a cross-country service back north. *Simon Bendall Collection*

LEFT: Some carriage sheds were little more than covered accommodation, offering no maintenance facilities. Such was the case at Llandudno Junction, which was used for a time for the storage of surplus stock. This included the two Metro-Cammell Class 151 prototypes, 151004 and 151003, which were pictured on May 30, 1990. *Simon Bendall Collection*

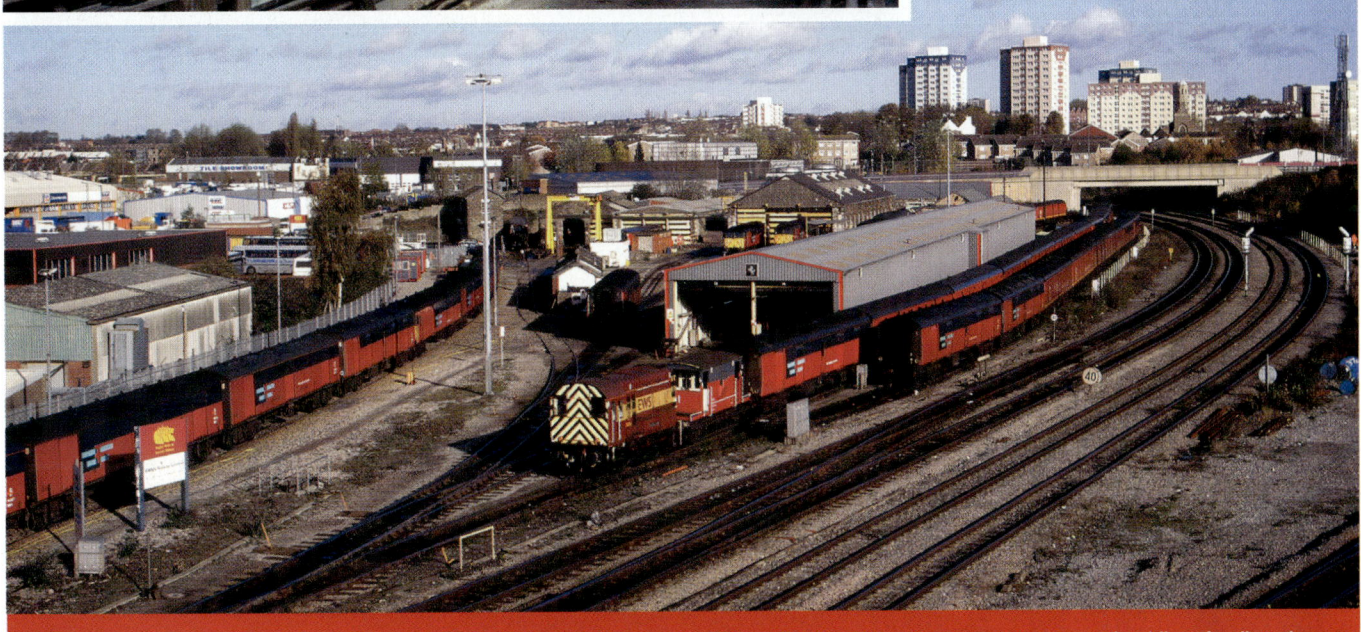

ABOVE: An overview of Bristol Barton Hill in 2000 following its refurbishment by EWS and while still used for the maintenance and stabling of mail stock. The grey two-road shed was the principal new addition while a fuelling point was also added, which can be glimpsed by the two Class 47s. Today, the depot is operated by Arriva Traincare and mostly used for the servicing of CrossCountry 'Voyagers' and multiple unit overhauls. *Simon Bendall Collection*

Modelling BR: Diesel Depots 41

Diesel depot development

Depots from the air

There is no better way to get an appreciation for the layout of maintenance depots than from above, this showing the track layout, building scale and ancillary features. Thanks to the drone photography of Rob Higgins, a selection of current day sheds is pictured in this manner.

ABOVE: DB Cargo, and EWS before it, has long concentrated maintenance activities on Toton, closing most of its other large depots across the country in favour of mobile maintenance staff working out of vans. As well as its own locos, DB carries out maintenance for other operators, most notably DC Rail and its sometimes temperamental Class 60s. Here Cappagh blue 60028 is lurking on the fuelling point on June 1, 2020, and a grey example to the north of the shed. Much of the main building is single ended while on the left are Network Rail's Sandiacre ballast sidings. *Rob Higgins*

LEFT: Direct Rail Services' depot at Crewe Gresty Bridge features extensively in this volume, not only because the various open days have made it easy to photograph, but also as it is a very modellable location, blending the old with the new. Plain blue 37422 and Mainline-liveried 37419 stand out from the crowd on September 20, 2019, alongside classmates, two '20/3s', a '66', two '68s' and an '88'. The blue-painted extension to the shed is obvious while the other blue building contains stores, particularly for the Stadler-built classes. Next to this is the office and staff block. *Rob Higgins*

Diesel depot development

ABOVE: **Freightliner's depot at Leeds Midland Road** has grown significantly since it was built on the site of an aggregates terminal, including adding a wheel lathe and the lifting gantry, which was subsequently enclosed in its own taller building. It does remain a cramped site though, especially with the row of stored Class 70s taking up space along the main line as 47815 passes by on May 13, 2022, with empty charter stock to Norwich. 59005 stands out amid the sea of green while present for a bogie overhaul. *Rob Higgins*

ABOVE: **Freightliner's second main depot was established at Crewe Basford Hall**, just across the road from Gresty Bridge, in 2016 and is seen two years later on August 27, 2018. On the left is Network Rail's track recycling centre with Crewe Coal Sidings above the shed building, this secure compound being used by DRS for nuclear flask stabling. Most Freightliner traction still stables within Basford Hall yard, leaving the depot free for maintenance. Virgin-liveried spare parts donor 86251 is in the foreground. *Rob Higgins*

ABOVE: The compact Electro-Motive Diesels facility at Longport, Stoke, is a particularly interesting case as it acts as an independent maintenance centre for all General Motors products in the UK. As a result, locos from pretty much all of the freight companies can be seen rubbing shoulders, making it something of a modeller's dream. On August 15, 2018, hood-less 66735 is shunted by 08220 while an assortment of Class 56s is stabled for conversion into Class 69s and the battered shell of 66048 awaits an overdue date with a gas-axe. *Rob Higgins*

ABOVE: Home to the West Midlands Class 323 fleet, Soho depot in Birmingham barely registers for many, given its near exclusive diet of EMUs. The depot was almost deserted on October 10, 2020, except for a couple of Class 323s hiding behind the shed and resident pilot 08805, which is largely retained to move bogies about during unit overhauls. However, the depot is relatively compact and offers inspiration for anyone considering a multiple unit facility. In addition, the long disused depot fuelling point in the foreground was recommissioned in August 2023. *Rob Higgins*

Diesel depot development

An ode to Western Road

Few layouts have evoked the spirit of a Western Region shed in the 1970s better than Western Road. Ian Manderson presents two further views of Mike Anson's work, again with guest diesel hydraulics from the late Pete Johnson's Canada Road.

ABOVE: In a view that will rekindle memories for anyone that has stood on the footbridge at Canton or looked down over Bath Road, three types of diesel-hydraulic traction are prominent in this scene across the depot yard. Pre-dating the release of the Dapol Class 22 is D6333, which is an extensive re-working of the ancient Hornby Class 21/29 hybrid. Joining it are 'Hymeks' D7005 in BR green, which went to its grave without receiving blue, and 7076, now preserved at the East Lancashire Railway. The Class 35 still ranks as one of Heljan's best models, despite it also being one of its earliest. Ian Manderson

Looking every inch at home among the outstanding scratchbuilt Western Region structures, the various hydraulics slumber under blue skies as they await the start of a new working week or, perhaps, the end of yet another industrial dispute! The skyline is dominated to either side by the water tower and maintenance building with the three-road servicing shed between them, all the structures being scratchbuilt. Ian Manderson

Modelling BR: Diesel Depots 45

Diesel depot development

Electrics at home

While this volume of *Modelling British Railways* is entitled Diesel Depots, electric locos require maintenance too. Inspired by Crewe Electric, James Makin duly built Wells Green TMD to allow both his diesel and electric fleets to be exhibited.

I have always been fascinated by overhead electrification, in particular the Mk.1 style of 25kV AC catenary used on the southern half of the West Coast Main Line, thanks to the massive gantries spanning multiple tracks and the complicated wiring at junctions. So, when the Diesel & Electric Modellers United society announced a small layout competition for 2005, I jumped at the chance to tackle something AC electric themed.

The inspiration for Wells Green TMD came from Crewe Electric as I wanted to produce something a little more unusual in OO gauge than the typical stabling point. I instead opted to portray a small section of a larger depot due to the space restrictions of the competition, with scenic hints to the larger facility beyond.

Starting with the backscene, this was split into three sections consisting of an administration block, a low-relief maintenance building and a half-relief four road servicing shed, These were all scratchbuilt from various parts with sections of Pikestuff kits mixed together with Wills sheets and styrene strip. To make the depot look bigger than it is, there are fully-lit rooms modelled behind the backscene, including a meeting room in the admin block.

This idea was expanded further for the low relief maintenance building as behind the large, glazed windows, there is space for a spare loco to be left, this giving the appearance that it is receiving attention and suggesting the depot is much larger than what is on view. Moving to the catenary, this utilises the 4mm scale gantry kits available from N Brass Locomotives along with fishing wire and Sommerfeldt sections for the wiring.

One of my main objectives for Wells Green was to portray a run-down atmosphere with the infrastructure and surroundings in poor condition, similar to the condition of many of today's neglected railway sites. This is something that is often not represented so helps set the layout apart. Graffiti was one of the easiest ways of depicting an urban environment, all of it being hand-painted

ABOVE: The centrepiece of the layout is the servicing shed, which is modelled in half-relief, this allows a single loco to be fully accommodated inside on each road. Three of the lines are grouped together in a Crewe Electric-style vista with the fourth in a separate building, the doorway being located above 66241. The portable building is the Knightwing kit with plenty of small details to take in. James Makin

ABOVE: Urban decay is an unfortunate fact of life in the 21st century and this is portrayed in full on Wells Green with graffiti aplenty, even on the odd loco. 66057 has arrived on shed to be cleaned after being targeted overnight. James Makin

46 www.keymodelworld.com

Diesel depot development

RIGHT: **Rail Express Systems-liveried 47736 *Cambridge Traction & Rolling Stock Depot*** pokes its cab into the fourth road of the servicing shed beneath the mass of overhead wires. The low-relief maintenance depot can be seen behind the Class 47, complete with the large picture windows to show off a loco placed behind the glazing. James Makin

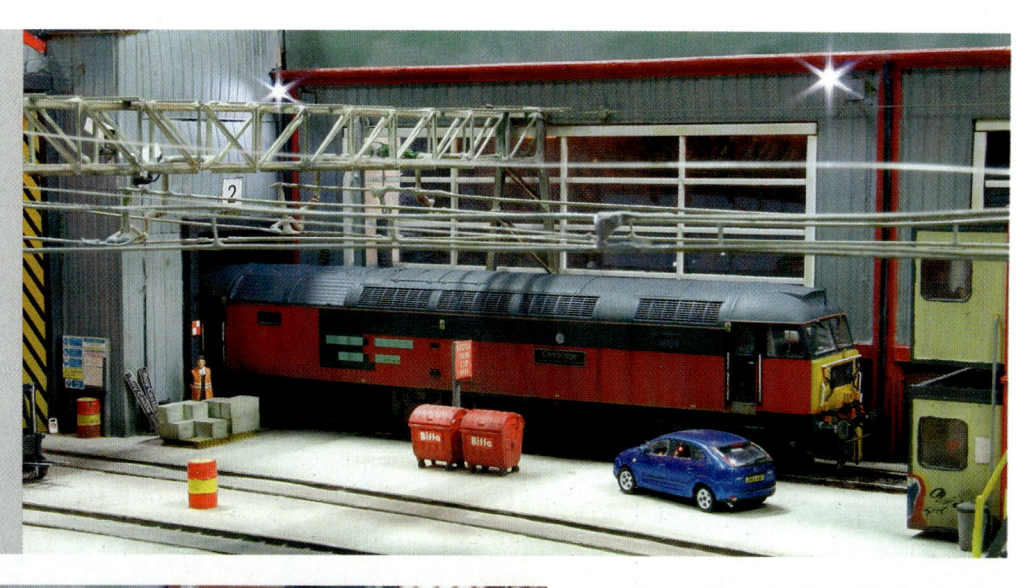

from photos. Clutter and lineside debris also abound as does a police unit investigating a crime scene, complete with forensic tent. This may not be to everyone's taste, but I am seeking to represent modern urban life not idyllic green countryside.

When the layout debuted, the electric locos were limited to reworked Hornby Class 86s and Class 90s along with Lima Class 92s alongside a selection of diesels. Nowadays, an all-new electric fleet is being assembled and expanded using the variety of high quality locos available from Accurascale, Bachmann, Heljan, and Hornby.

LEFT: **Railway operations continue despite the ongoing police incident as 47767 *Mappa Mundi* arrives on shed and passes sister 47831 in the washing plant. Looking on is Virgin's 86231 *Starlight Express.*** Above the diesels can be seen the exit road to the fiddle yard, which is hidden as much as possible by retaining walls. James Makin

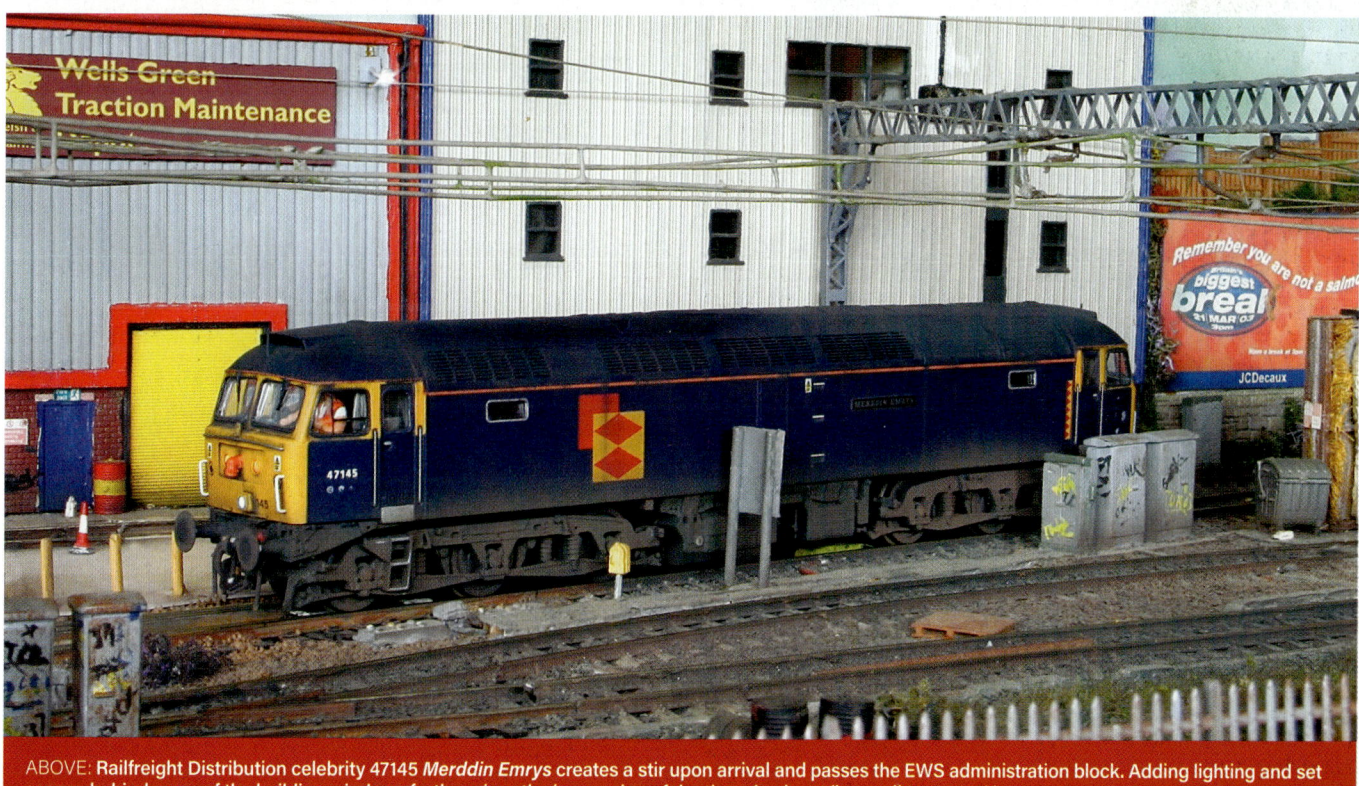

ABOVE: **Railfreight Distribution celebrity 47145 *Merddin Emrys* creates a stir upon arrival and passes the EWS administration block.** Adding lighting and set scenes behind some of the building windows further gives the impression of depth and a depot 'beyond'. James Makin

Modelling BR: Diesel Depots   **47**

SUBSCRIBE

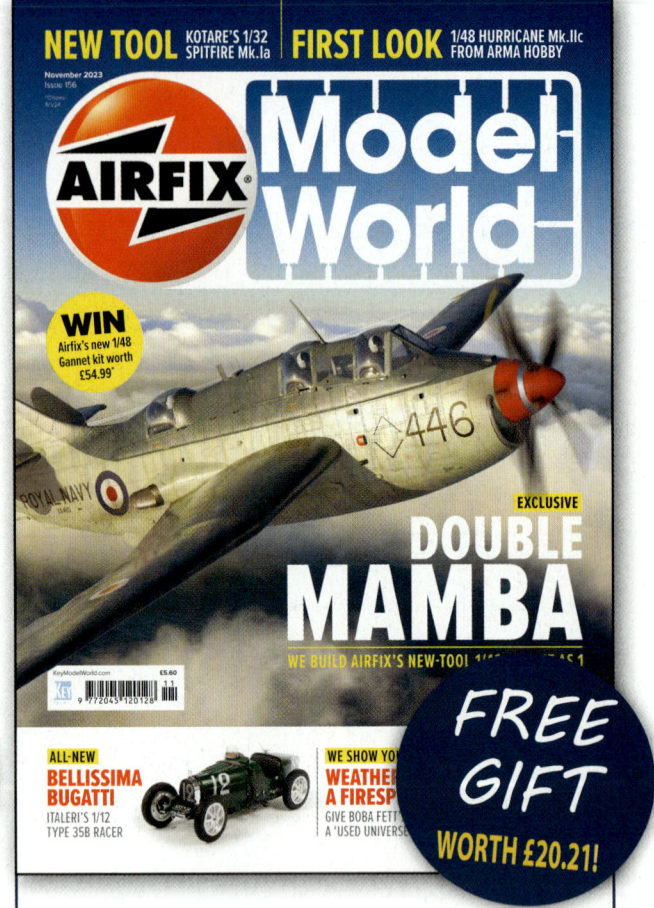

Written by modellers for modellers of all skill levels, *Hornby* magazine takes a unique approach to model railways

shop.keypublishing.com/hmsubs

Airfix Model World is your complete guide to the world of scale modelling. Published monthly, it caters for all manner of modellers.

shop.keypublishing.com/amwsubs

ORDER DIRECT FROM OUR SHOP...
shop.keypublish

OR CALL +44 (0)1780 480404

(Lines open 9.00-5.30, Monday-Friday GMT)

Key Publishing

704/23

TODAY

SAVE UP TO £42 WHEN YOU SUBSCRIBE!

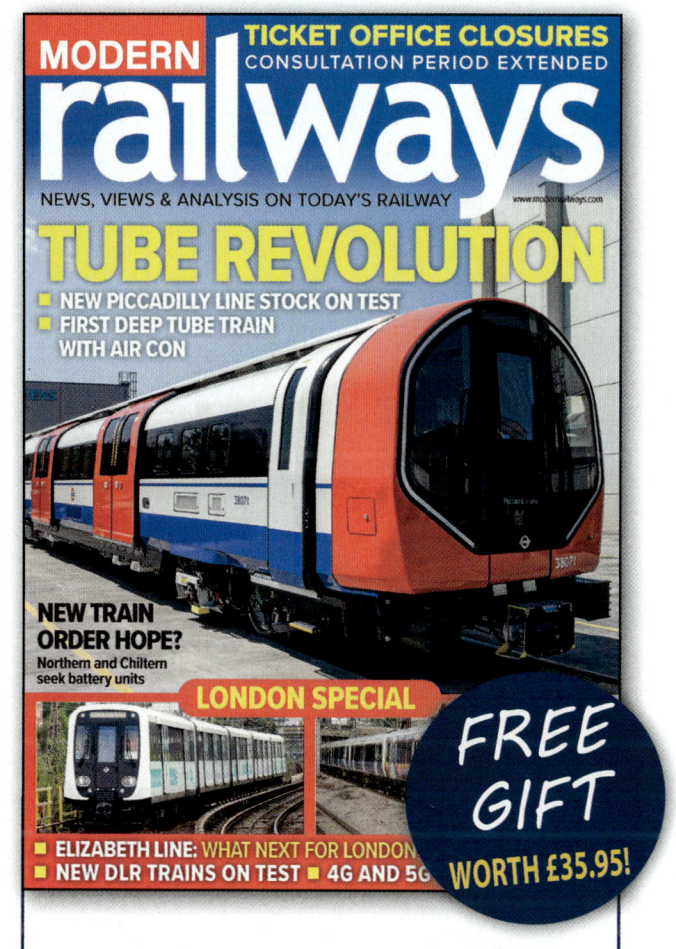

MODERN railways
NEWS, VIEWS & ANALYSIS ON TODAY'S RAILWAY

TICKET OFFICE CLOSURES — CONSULTATION PERIOD EXTENDED

TUBE REVOLUTION
- NEW PICCADILLY LINE STOCK ON TEST
- FIRST DEEP TUBE TRAIN WITH AIR CON

NEW TRAIN ORDER HOPE? Northern and Chiltern seek battery units

LONDON SPECIAL
- ELIZABETH LINE: WHAT NEXT FOR LONDON
- NEW DLR TRAINS ON TEST
- 4G AND 5G

FREE GIFT WORTH £35.95!

Published for over 50 years, **Modern Railways** has earned its reputation in the industry as an established and highly respected railway journal.

shop.keypublishing.com/mrsubs

MLI Plus
MODERN LOCOMOTIVES ILLUSTRATED
No. 262 — £7.99

SOUTHERN MODERNISATION – CLASS 455s

Chasing BRCW Type 2s

- Class 59s - The ARC Fleet
- Class 74 - The 'Big EDs'
- Rails in Sri Lanka
- MLI Plus Modellers' Review
- Mainline Freight
- Vivarail '230s' on Marston Vale

FREE GIFT WORTH £20.94!

The most informed partwork in UK rail is now even better. From issue 248, **Modern Locomotives Illustrated** became **MLI+** and it's bigger, brighter, and even more informative.

shop.keypublishing.com/mlisubs

Diesel depot development

Depot pits and flooring

Having examined the different types of depot building, Simon Bendall now begins a consideration of the interiors by looking at the basics, including inspection pits and raised walkways.

The shed building is just one part of creating a convincing depot layout, although for many detailing just the exterior is more than sufficient. However, if you do want to fit out the interior of your building, there are a considerable number of items to consider.

Starting with the basics, there are inspection pits and elevated walkways, different regions having a variety of preferences in both cases. Any TMD would have illuminated inspection pits installed under some or all of the maintenance roads, often for their full length. In some cases, the centre pit between the rails might be supplemented by side pits, either to the same depth or shallower, all having access steps at both ends.

For example, Western Region depots tended to have what could be considered a traditional pit with brick lining and sunken beneath the depot floor. In contrast, the Eastern Region preferred a more open approach with much of the depot floor beneath rail height, the rails instead being raised and supported on substantial metal posts bolted to the concrete. This gave more comprehensive access to all parts of the underframe but was more complex to construct, which applies in model form as well.

In the BR era, the pits were typically filthy places stained with oil, fuel, and dirt and, depending on the state of the drains, home to puddles. The lighting could either be proud of the pit walls or recessed into them and only as good as the maintenance allowed, especially in cleaning the plastic covers. Between the rails, metal walkways could usually be found to allow staff to cross the pit safely without walking round to the end.

Nowadays, health and safety legislation has ensured pits are much better looked after, the walls often being painted white and the floors dry. At many newer depots, the risk to staff of falling into pits is taken seriously with a variety of measures put in place, such as retractable ribbon barriers with posts that can be removed if required. It is not just pits that are better maintained nowadays, the floors in general being cleaner and tidier, and often painted rather than bare concrete. Red and blue are common colours with yellow close to pits, but the combinations vary from depot to depot.

Another aspect that varied between regions during the BR era was the provision of fixed raised walkways along the maintenance roads. Again, the Eastern Region favoured these down both sides of its maintenance bays, the walkways and support posts being made of concrete. Depots on other regions could have none, such as Old Oak Common, while others had a half and half approach, such as Toton. Again, some modern depots favour raised walkways on some roads, normally of steel mesh construction.

ABOVE: A typical scene at a TMD during the BR era as 37175 receives attention inside Eastfield in September 1990. As well as dirty floors and work-stained pits, the lighting is basic, while trolleys, containers, and parts litter the floor. The trolley in the foreground features two plastic containers, one of which is labelled fuel, while pallets of new brake blocks are to the left of it.
Simon Bendall Collection

Diesel depot development

LEFT: Following its transfer south from Eastfield, 37422 is seen undergoing engine repairs inside Tinsley in mid-1989. The raised walkways allowed staff level access to the locos, making it far easier to move tools and components around. Simon Bendall Collection

RIGHT: The downside of the Eastern Region approach was the sheer complexity of construction with support posts for the walkways and the elevated rails littering the sunken floor. Lighting was also installed beneath the walkways to illuminate the pit area. 56017 receives attention at Tinsley with two classmates in March 1986. Even with the walkways, portable gantries were still needed to access the roof, as seen to the right. Simon Bendall Collection

LEFT: Each raised walkway at Tinsley had steps provided at the outer ends by the shed doors as well as steps down into the pits, these framing 47118 in 1989 following transfer from Eastfield. For 4mm scale modellers, West Hill Wagon Works offers a comprehensive kit to model the Tinsley style of pits and walkways, over 120 parts combining to make the sunken floor, elevated rails and raised walkways. These also include the end steps, central access ladders and may other detailing parts. Simon Bendall Collection

RIGHT: The inside of the servicing and fuelling shed at Old Oak Common is seen on December 27, 2008, this being the view towards the turntable. Partial central pits are provided but the red floor and white safety lines are largely lost beneath the grime. Amongst the many details to be observed are the roof-mounted heating elements, ducting to channel the exhaust fumes, personal doors for access and fire escape, and the assortment of wall-mounted electrical conduit. Simon Bendall

Modelling BR: Diesel Depots 51

Diesel depot development

ABOVE: **Admittedly taken when the depot was months from closure and building maintenance had ceased, a pit inside the Factory at Old Oak Common on August 2, 2008, does not look particularly inviting. While the access steps and drainage may have been fixed on a fully functioning depot, the general condition was not atypical.** Simon Bendall

ABOVE: **A closer look at the Factory pit shows useful details, such as the wheel stops bolted to the rail ends, slatted metal steps for drainage and the method of rail fixing.** Simon Bendall

ABOVE AND BELOW: **The short pit at Crewe Gresty Bridge in 2012 is a marked contrast to the West London depot, being reasonably clean and at least dry. Yellow paint highlights the pit edges with red used for the rest of the floor. A mix of concrete and metal mesh steps provide access.** Simon Bendall

ABOVE: **The modern method for protecting pits at several depots is to install the retractable ribbons typically used for queue control, complete with 'Beware open pit' warnings. The posts are removable so can be lifted out when required. 86628 stands amid a forest of ribbons at the then newly completed and pristine Crewe Basford Hall depot of Freightliner on November 11, 2016.** Simon Bendall

Diesel depot development

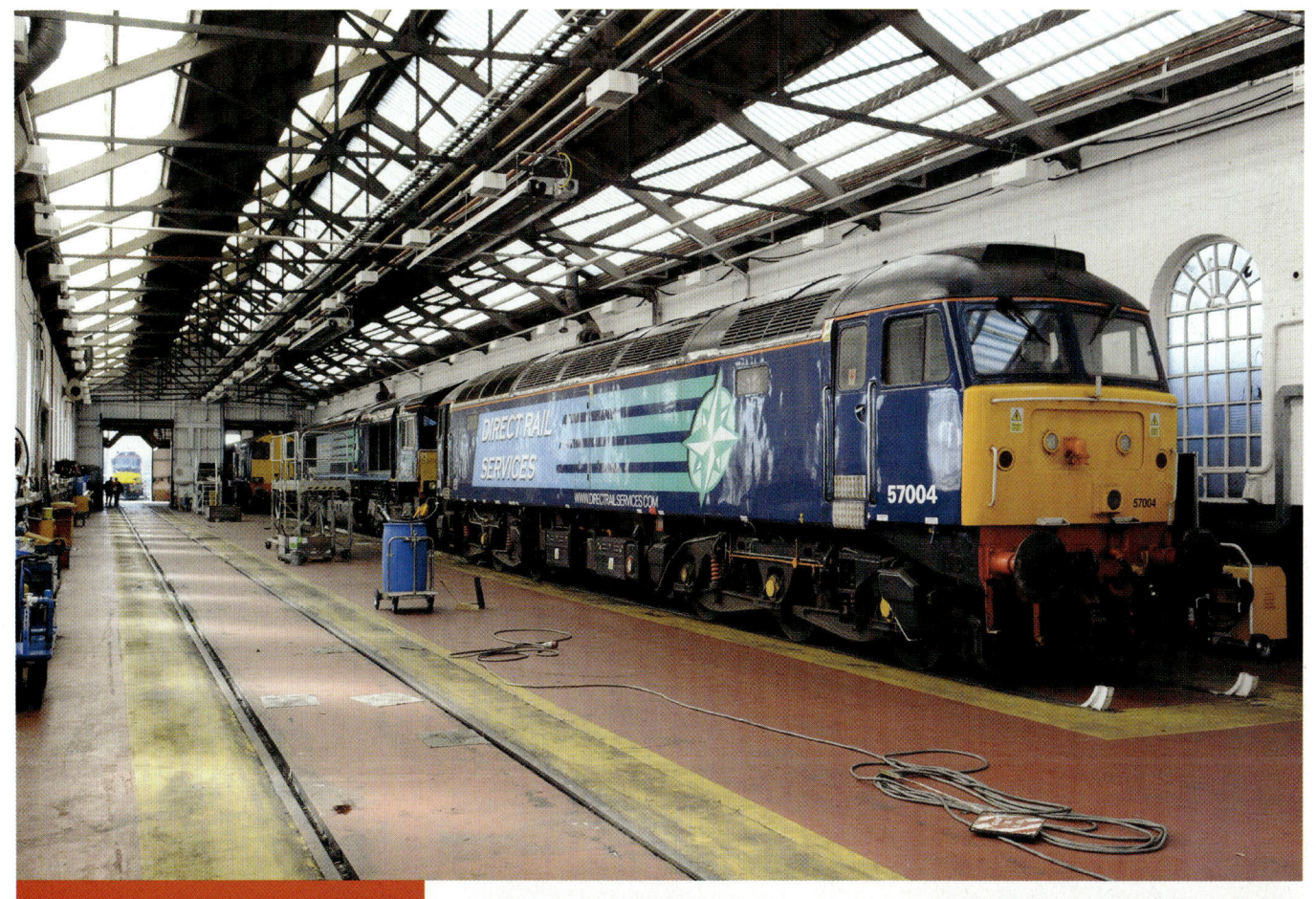

ABOVE: **A general view of the interior and floor of Crewe Gresty Bridge on March 11, 2014, as a brand new 68002** *Intrepid* **is displayed to the media through the open doorway in the distance. Undergoing attention are 57004, 66423 and 20302, the Class 66 receiving repairs to minor bodyside scrape damage.** Simon Bendall

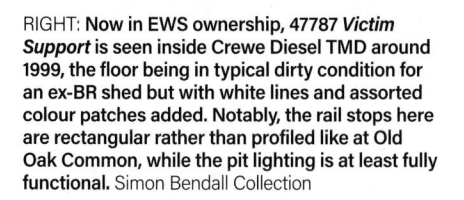

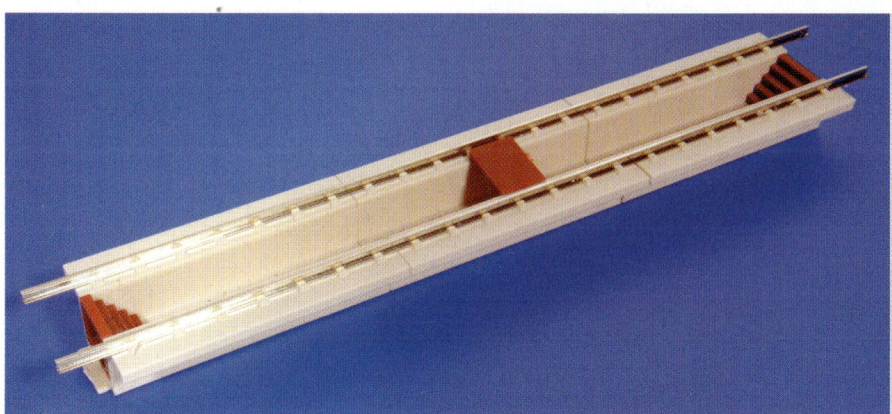

RIGHT: **Now in EWS ownership, 47787** *Victim Support* **is seen inside Crewe Diesel TMD around 1999, the floor being in typical dirty condition for an ex-BR shed but with white lines and assorted colour patches added. Notably, the rail stops here are rectangular rather than profiled like at Old Oak Common, while the pit lighting is at least fully functional.** Simon Bendall Collection

LEFT: **For many modellers looking to add an inspection pit to their depot, the first and only port of call will be Peco, which offers a kit in both N and OO. In fact, two versions are available in OO gauge to take account of the different rail fixings needed for either Code 75 or Code 100 rail. The pit itself is moulded in beige plastic and modular in nature, the short 50mm sections allowing any length to be assembled. Two sets of end steps and three cross-pit walkways are supplied in each pack along with the lengths of rail. While perfectly adequate for the purpose, it lacks any representation of the wall lighting. An alternative supplier in N gauge only is West Hill Wagon Works, where a simple plastic kit is available to create an inspection pit in two lengths.**

Modelling BR: Diesel Depots 53

Diesel depot development

Homemade inspection pits by Terry Bendall

ABOVE: A view of the pit installation in progress with the aperture cut out for one pit and an assembled pit and steps being test fitted into another. Any gaps that result around the edges can be filled in.

A cheaper alternative to using the Peco inspection pits is to make your own, something that is particularly necessary if working in either EM or P4 gauges as the Peco mouldings are unsuitable for the wider track spacing without modification. Pictured here is one way to do this as well as creating and weathering the floor of a TMD to represent a typically filthy BR condition in the 1980s.

The top of the baseboards were made from 9mm thick plywood, this thickness being chosen to make it a bit easier to cut the slots. These were marked out and an 8mm diameter hole was drilled close to each end, this allowing the blade of a portable electric jig saw to be used to remove the bulk of the waste wood. Trimming back to the lines was mainly done with a file but a wood chisel was used in places. Glass paper wrapped round a thin strip of wood was then used to smooth the cut surfaces. The slots were made wide enough to allow the wooden sides of the pits to be slid into place, so they were level with the top surface of the baseboard.

The pits themselves were made from thin strips of wood with the side walls being 25mm by 4mm and the floor pieces being 16mm by 8mm. This ensured that the walls were the correct distance apart to support the rails. On this model, the track was built to P4 standards with a track gauge of 18.83mm so the distance between the pit walls had to allow for this. If OO gauge track is used, then the distance between the walls would have to be reduced. The sides were fixed to the floor using PVA woodworking glue with some small panel pins used to hold things while the glue dried. A coat of white wood primer was applied to the wood, and this was followed by two coats of Humbrol No.103.

To fix the pits to the baseboard, some strips of wood, 30mm by 8mm, were cut to length to span the space across the tracks below the baseboard top. These had slots cut in them to fit over the assembled pits and these were then screwed in place from below the baseboard to support the pits in the correct position. The steps were made from 2mm thick styrene sheet cut into strips of varying width with the bottom step being the widest, the rest being built up from there.

Adding the rails

A consultation of photos showed that many depots employed flat bottom rail on pit roads, so suitable rail was obtained from the Scalefour Society stores. On the prototype, a range of track fixings are used so for this model, a clamp type was employed. These were made using 20 thou thick brass sheet cut from scrap etches, measuring 2.5mm long by 1.5mm wide. These were soldered to the rails at appropriate intervals and a clamp plate made up by creating a right angled bend in a strip of 1mm wide brass and cutting a piece 1mm long from it. This was then soldered in place. While a very fiddly and time consuming task, it is only required on the inner side of each rail as the outer side will be hidden under the depot floor.

The ends of the pit rails were joined using copper-clad sleepers, again since these would be hidden under the floor, with the all-important insulation gap being cut in the copper and checked before the sleepers were soldered in place. Check rails were soldered to the copper-clad sleepers at the ends since on the prototype, these would be needed to retain the concrete floor and this arrangement was extended outside the shed where the concrete apron would be created.

In order to get the pit rails at the correct height to match the sleepers, strips of styrene were glued to the top of the pit walls. The rails were then fixed to these strips using superglue with track gauges

ABOVE: The clamp type fixings used for the rails along the pits can be seen along with the styrene strip packing underneath. The copper-clad sleepers give rigidity as the track is soldered to them, as are the check rails.

Diesel depot development

ABOVE: The two lines at the bottom of the picture will be inside the shed building but without pits so are laid on cooper-clad sleepers, the wider spacing saving on materials and invisible once the depot floor was laid. The checkrails can also be seen, while the rail sides and chairs are also receiving a suitably rusty finish.

being used to hold the rails in place and to the correct gauge while the glue dried.

Some of the shed roads were designed to be without pits so the track for these was flat bottom rail soldered to copper-clad sleepers. No track fixings were modelled on these lines since everything would be hidden by the floor, which is why the sleeper spacing was also increased. Check rails were again fitted along the whole length of these rails for the concrete infills as was done for the apron sections. Once all of this was in place, the rest of the track that would be outside of the shed was laid, wired-up and tested to make sure everything worked before the floor of the shed was laid. Some styrene packing was necessary to ensure that the track was level throughout the shed and out onto the rest of the baseboard, where the track was laid on cork underlay.

Making the floor
The floor of the shed building was made from styrene sheet of various thicknesses. The start of the process was to cut 40 thou thick styrene into strips about 20mm wide and these were glued to the top of the baseboard using an impact adhesive. Further strips were also placed each side of the tracks with additional ones where the gap was sufficiently wide to require extra support.

These strips all acted as supports for the shed floor itself and to help raise the level to match the height of the rails. Pieces of 80 thou thick sheet were then cut and fitted on top of the packing pieces, taking care to ensure they were neither above or below the tops of the rails. These pieces were also made as large as practicable to reduce the number of joints needed and were fixed in place using polystyrene cement.

Gaps had to be left to allow the walls of the shed building to fit between the sheets so it could be bedded in. At the same time, strips of styrene were cut to fit between the rails, and these were extended to form part of the apron outside the shed walls. Any gaps in the sheets were filled with a suitable model filler and sanded smooth when hardened. The remaining areas of concrete outside the shed walls were created after the building had been temporarily put in place so that the sheets could be butted up to the shed walls.

Painting and weathering
A lot of time was spent in looking at pictures of shed floors from the BR era in order to get an appropriate colour and finish for the model. The base coat was Humbrol No.103 applied with a wide brush and, when dry, a range of dark greys and browns were used to create an oil and dirt stained appearance. The various colours were mixed on a small palette and applied as a fairly dry mix with a stippling effect in a circular motion using a fairly wide brush with short bristles.

When the brush needed re-charging, new colours were added in different proportions to vary the density of the finish. Where the colour was felt to be incorrect, it was removed using a clean brush dipped in thinners and then re-applied. A rust colour was applied to the edges of the rails using a finer brush. When everything was dry, a thin wash of Railmatch No.405 sleeper grime was applied to tone things down and even up the density of colour where needed.

ABOVE: The floor of the shed building is seen largely in place, it features two dead-end half-length roads with pits, two through roads also with pits and two more through roads without pits.

ABOVE: Pictures showed that unsurprisingly the floors tended to be dirtiest between the rails and nearest to them, so the colours were varied to match. At this point, the rail heads had yet to be cleaned up, while the clean plastic is the exterior shed apron and yet to be weathered. The notches for the shed walls can also be seen.

Modelling BR: Diesel Depots 55

Diesel depot development

Lifting jacks

The ability to perform locomotive lifts to undertake bogie changes and other repairs is a fundamental role of a TMD. Simon Bendall looks at both the prototype and modelling options.

Being able to lift a locomotive to undertake maintenance has been a fundamental requirement of the railways since they were invented. Whereas overhead cranes and end-on lifting hoists were favoured for steam locos, the latter were of little use for diesels. Instead, lifting jacks were developed, these making use of the substantial frames of diesel locos to lift on all four corners simultaneously. With the loco securely suspended in mid-air, bogies can then be rolled out for attention to wheelsets, traction motors and any other components. Additionally, with the bogies out of the way, the body can be lowered again over a pit to give access to the fuel tank, chassis pipework, and other underslung equipment.

ABOVE: The heavy lift area of the Factory plays host to 50003 *Temeraire* around 1990 as it waits to undergo a body lift at Old Oak Common. Supplied by Matterson Cranes, the four jacks are more substantial than some other types employed by BR at the time. The rack of drums to the right is an interesting feature while the storage cage in the foreground contains brake blocks. Simon Bendall Collection

ABOVE: A Type 5 line-up at Toton on March 6, 1994, as the privatisation process was about to take effect. 56058 has been lifted and both bogies rolled out while 58008 and 60075 look on. Of note are the bogie springs for the 'Grid' sitting on the floor by the jack and the disconnected traction motor cables hanging down beneath the loco. Simon Bendall Collection

A number of manufacturers supplied lifting jacks to BR over the years and while there was some variation in size, the basic arrangement was the same. Typically, the jacks were also wheeled or provided with trollies, allowing them to be positioned to suit different lengths of loco. In more recent years, computer-controlled synchronised lifting jacks have been introduced to allow complete multiple units to be lifted, thereby avoiding having to uncouple and split individual cars, something that is best avoided these days with the mass of jumper cable connections between them. However, lifting a complete unit of four or more cars does have its risks and a handful of units have suffered serious damage over the years when the jacks lifting one car have failed while the adjacent car remained raised.

www.keymodelworld.com

Diesel depot development

RIGHT: Now in EWS ownership, 31273 had been lifted almost as high as possible at Crewe Diesel in 1996, demonstrating the need for a TMD building to have good height clearance. The wheeled nature of the jacks is evident with pallet truck-style handles integrated into them. The 'Not to be moved' sign on the front of the Class 31 is a tad redundant as 37116 *Sister Dora* looks on.
Simon Bendall Collection

LEFT: InterCity Swallow-liveried 47520 had also been lifted at Crewe Diesel in 1995, it now being part of the Rail Express Systems fleet. With the bogie at the No.1 end rolled out, the body had been lowered again to sit just above the other bogie, easing the strain on the jacks and generally making things safer. Having seen a loco lift go wrong, it is not something you want to be close to!
Simon Bendall Collection

RIGHT: Recently repainted in BR green, a yet to be named 37411 grabs some air, the presence of the miniature snowploughs ensuring the loco has to be particularly high for the bogies to pass underneath them. The lifting jacks look to be on the verge of replacement with modern versions to the left, their motors still covered in plastic on the tops. The difference in size is considerable!
Simon Bendall Collection

Modelling BR: Diesel Depots 57

Diesel depot development

ABOVE: **During the Old Oak Common open day on September 2, 2017, 57603** *Tintagel Castle* **was recorded on the Somers lifting jacks in the heavy repair shop of the Great Western depot with prototype HST power car 41001 alongside. This building had been constructed some 15 years earlier to provide major repair facilities at the London end of the company's route, where previously there had been none. However, at the end of 2018, it along with the rest of the Great Western depot would be closed to allow for construction of the HS2 station, with maintenance transferring across to the former Eurostar depot at North Pole.** Simon Bendall

BELOW: **A rarely pictured depot is Northampton Kings Heath, the home of the Class 350 fleet used by London Northwestern. On December 11, 2017, the company had just taken over the franchise from London Midland and was unveiling its new livery. Units on shed that day included 350256 which is seen on the jacking road in the still largely pristine depot, despite the Siemens facility having opened over 11 years earlier. In contrast to the central pit the 'Desiro' is over, the adjacent road has side pits as well with the rails on raised concrete supports.** Simon Bendall

ABOVE: **Another open day, this time at Derby Etches Park on September 13, 2014, found 222104 on display while the synchronised jacks lifted all four cars. Illustrating the risks of this practice, sister unit 222103 spent almost two years out of traffic after the lifting jacks failed under one driving coach during a lift at Crofton in January 2007, causing considerable damage to the inner end of the vehicle as it was securely attached to the adjacent car.** Simon Bendall

Diesel depot development

LEFT: A comparison with the Class 50 picture on page 56 shows that not a huge amount had changed inside the Factory despite the passage of some 18 years when 66050 was recorded at Old Oak Common on August 2, 2008. The jacks have received a repaint into red but are still the same ones, while the walls are dirtier with more peeling paint. This was one of the final locos to receive heavy maintenance at the depot, some of the brake pipework having been disconnected from the bogie and laid behind it. The shot also provides a good view of the array of electrical and fuse cabinets on the wall, complete with roof and guttering to protect them from a leaky roof! The classic but long broken Network SouthEast clock hanging from the roof is a reminder of a previous depot operator.
Simon Bendall

ABOVE: The lifting jacks at Crewe Gresty Bridge had been moved alongside the shed wall, but clear of the fire door, for the duration of the open day on July 10, 2010. In keeping with modern safety standards, the red and white limited clearance signs can sometimes be seen adorning the jack superstructure.
Simon Bendall

ABOVE: Bachmann has offered lifting jacks in its Scenecraft range in both 4mm and 7mm, the latter being pictured. Finished in mustard yellow with a wash of weathering, the lifting arms are a push fit and can be positioned at a variety of heights. Although nicely moulded, there is scope to add further details such as motors.

ABOVE LEFT AND ABOVE RIGHT: Among the suppliers of 3D printed parts, Rusty Rails Modelling offers a set of four jacks in 4mm scale, these coming as one piece prints that just require painting. Pictured as supplied out of the packet and then painted up, several coats of yellow are required to get coverage, after which the details can be picked out in various colours based on pictures. Restricted clearance notices were added, in this case from an ancient Lineside Look sheet. Of note is that the Rusty Rails logo is included on the side of each jack, which you may wish to fill and rub down.

Modelling BR: Diesel Depots 59

Diesel depot development

Overhead cranes

Another common feature at major TMDs is an overhead crane to carry out power unit changes, although these are not always found inside the building as Simon Bendall explains.

ABOVE: A number of depots had a crane installed outside of the buildings, such as at Cardiff Canton where 08375 and 37884 were among the locos stabled by it on May 27, 1990. Rated to lift a maximum of 50 tonnes, this was more than sufficient for a complete power unit. *Simon Bendall Collection*

When the new generation of diesel maintenance depots were constructed in the 1960s, opinions differed between regions on whether they should be provided with heavy lift capabilities. Some management theorised that such work was the purview of the main workshops and locos requiring a power unit change could be hauled to the works to be attended to. Others took a more enlightened view and equipped their depots with an overhead crane, deeming that it would be quicker and easier to do the work at depot level.

However, a depot typically had to be designed with a crane in mind from the outset, allowing the building to be tall enough to have sufficient clearance get a power unit over a loco. Cranes were not just used for engine lifts, given that most major components on a diesel loco are heavy and bulky, therefore needing to come out through a roof hatch or with the roof panel completely removed. The radiator fan, radiators, generator, and traction motor blowers are just some of the items that typically need to go in from above.

For depots without an overhead crane, it could be good practice for the breakdown crane gang undertaking lifts outside, while at others external gantry cranes were erected at later dates as facilities were upgraded. Privatisation saw a number of train operating companies, both freight and passenger, invest in their depot infrastructure so they were as self-sufficient as possible, especially as the number of main workshops went into decline.

RIGHT: Sixteen cylinders of English Electric majesty are hoisted aloft at Old Oak Common on November 22, 2008, as the rebuilt 16CSVT engine is reinstalled in 50026 *Indomitable*. Built 104 years earlier, the Factory was not designed with such lifts in mind with clearances being particularly tight over the roof of the loco. The crane operator can be seen in white overalls in his perch above the lifting beam as the elderly equipment clanked about. 47847 stands alongside on the right. *Simon Bendall*

Diesel depot development

LEFT: At Laira, a gantry crane was provided above the repair bays and their elevated work platforms. In May 1989, 50002 *Superb* receives engine repairs with its central roof section removed. To the left, the steps down to the sunken floor and side and central pits can be seen, this part of Laira being arranged in a similar fashion to Tinsley. *Simon Bendall Collection*

ABOVE: Prior to Direct Rail Services taking over Gresty Bridge depot, it had been used for maintaining track machines and only featured fairly basic facilities. Amongst the equipment inherited was this fixed position hoist rated to lift 10 tonnes, which is seen at the depot open day on July 19, 2008, with 47501 having been named *Craftsman* earlier in the day. With DRS progressively improving the facilities at the depot, it was dismantled within a few years. *Simon Bendall*

ABOVE: Chiltern Railways invested in its Aylesbury depot in the mid-2000s to add a wheel lathe and lifting capability. However, with the depot situated on a rather cramped site, the crane had to be installed in the original shed dating from 1992 with the support beam coming through the side of the building and over one of the stabling roads. The resulting hole in the shed was provided with two doors, which are seen open behind 67015 *David J Lloyd* on October 10, 2009. *Simon Bendall*

BELOW: No height constraints exist in Freightliner's Crewe Basford Hall depot where a 25 tonne rated gantry crane is provided above two of the roads. 66614 *Poppy 1916-2016* is open for inspection by invited guests on November 11, 2016, for Remembrance Day. The safety ribbons around the pits can again be seen, particularly their distance from the actual drop. *Simon Bendall*

ABOVE: Recently released by Goodwood Scenics is a replica of the gantry crane that has stood outside the south end of Bescot TMD for many years, be it the original diesel depot or the current 'tin shed'. Measuring 118mm high and 150mm long, the fully finished structure is made to order and priced £119.95. *Goodwood Scenics*

Modelling BR: Diesel Depots **61**

Diesel depot development

Inspection gantries

With the popularity of depot layouts featuring DRS traction, **Simon Bendall** takes a look at the elevated inspection gantries that have been installed at both the company's depots.

Roof level elevated walkways have become increasing common in depots since privatisation, particularly those dealing with passenger stock, where regular access needs to be given to maintain air-conditioning units, pantographs, and other roof-mounted equipment. In contrast, they remain relatively unusual at freight depots, where loco roofs generally do not need to be accessed often and when they do, a portable gantry will do the job.

However, Direct Rail Services has bucked this trend at both its maintenance depots at Carlisle Kingmoor and Crewe Gresty Bridge, installing raised walkways on both sides of a depot road with linking bridges between them that go up and over the loco roof. Installed over a decade ago, they seemed like a belts and braces approach to maintenance at the time but now with Class 68s and Class 88s on the books, they give access to the pantograph on the latter and the cab roof air conditioning units on both.

ABOVE: With an extension to Gresty Bridge completed by July 2010, this allowed major repairs to be carried out for the first time with the installation of an overhead crane and, dominating the new space, an elevated walkway to give easy roof level access. At that month's open day, Stobart Rail-liveried 66411 *Eddie the Engine* stands beneath the new equipment. Simon Bendall

RIGHT: Moving round to the other side of 66411 reveals the stairs to the walkways as well as the lifting frame that has been used by the crane to remove the loco's hood section, giving access to the General Motors power unit. Tucked beneath the steps are pallet loads of bagged loco sand. Simon Bendall

Diesel depot development

RIGHT: Outside of an open day, the gantry at Crewe can be seen in full with the two sides linked by a bridge at each end, while two strengthening beams connect the far side legs to the shed wall. With no public to contend with, the shed floor is far less tidy! Simon Bendall

LEFT: Moving to the other end of the same pit road finds 66426 on the lifting jacks and with a wheelset removed, Cabinets, shelving and bins line the right hand wall with a forklift also poking into view. The area above is just as cluttered with vents, pipework and building struts. Simon Bendall

ABOVE: Looking like an exercise in Meccano, the elevated walkways at Kingmoor are far more complex, having both lower and upper levels on each side along with separate steps to access. On top of this is a gantry crane which, like the one at Crewe, is operated by remote control. This all sits between the pit road and roof beams, giving a somewhat shoehorned look, as seen during the depot open day on July 16, 2011. Simon Bendall

LEFT: Kingmoor is also home to a second gantry crane, its legs being visible in the previous shot. This view of 20308 on July 7, 2007, gives a better look at the Konecranes installation, which has a lift capacity of 10 tonnes. Simon Bendall

Modelling BR: Diesel Depots

KEY MODEL WORLD

YOUR ONLINE MODELLING

Unmissable modelling inspiration at your finger tips

"A modeller's paradise"
Christopher

"The key that unlocks the world of modelling!"
Graham

- ✓ Get all the **latest news** first
- ✓ **Exclusive** product and layout videos
- ✓ Fresh **inspiration**, tips and tricks every day
- ✓ More than **5,000 searchable** modelling articles
- ✓ Back issues of **Hornby magazine**
- ✓ Full access to **Hornby magazine** content
- ✓ All available on **any device** - *anywhere, anytime*

Visit:
www.keymod

SCALE ➤➤ DESTINATION

Featuring **HORNBY** magazine

AIRFIX Model World

FULL DEPOT BUILD SERIES AVAILBLE NOW!

EPISODE ONE: Baseboards, track and construction
In part one of our new diesel depot layout construction video series the team start by building the baseboards, laying the track and bringing the layout to life as the team introduce Natford TMD.

EPISODE TWO: Scenic development
In part two we continue Natford's journey as we create the basis of the ground cover, add ballast, weather the track and prepare the ground work for the scenic break.

EPISODE THREE: All about the details
In part three we focus on the details of the depot scene by adding a backscene using new products from Sankey Scenics, detailed ground cover, accessories and the first collection of rolling stock with a Scottish Region theme.

EPISODE FOUR: Lighting the way
In the fourth and final part the team add character to Natford TMD by installing interior lighting in the main depot building, connecting the yard lighting towers and adding ground signals at the depot entrance to complete our build.

Visit www.keymodelworld.com/building-a-diesel-depot to watch the full series

elworld.com

Fuelling points

Fuelling points

An essential feature of any depot layout, Simon Bendall examines the different styles of fuelling point employed by both British Rail and the privatised companies.

As already established, providing fuelling facilities for a diesel fleet is the most basic requirement of a maintenance facility, and the same should be true of a layout portraying one. As a result, most BR depots that were more than a mere stabling point could fuel locos but the manner in which this was achieved varied greatly.

The most familiar method was the external fuelling points favoured by the likes of the London Midland and North Eastern regions. Here, a pump would typically be sited between two tracks and capable of fuelling a loco on both sides simultaneously. To give some measure of weather protection, a canopy supported by two posts would be provided, from which electric strip lights hung. This canopy either angled upwards from the centre line on each side to give a 'v' shape or, as preferred by the North Eastern Region, was flat with rounded ends. The latter was of pre-cast concrete construction as were the posts, while steel was the normal material for the 'v' shape canopy and posts.

This was the BR fuelling point at its most basic, but the fixtures and fittings would vary from depot to depot. Invariably there would be some degree of pipework and shut off valves near the pump, and maybe a water supply available for hosing down. In later years, a portable fire extinguisher would be housed in a cabinet or, today, the plastic equivalent. The ground around the pump was invariably concrete and heavily stained with oil. The rails could also be directly fixed to concrete pads to create an apron, sometimes with absorbent matting both in between the rails and on the outside edges. Designs varied but it was uncommon to find properly ballasted and sleepered track by a fuelling point.

In contrast to the external fuelling points, both the Eastern and Western regions sometimes preferred to locate their fuelling points inside servicing sheds, where other maintenance activities and lower level exams could be carried out simultaneously. These could have fuel pumps serving three or four roads depending on the layout and the number of locos the depot was expected to service. The Scottish Region also made use of fuelling sheds at some depots, such as Eastfield, but these tended to be smaller, while other depots had little more than corrugated lean-to shelters.

ABOVE: **What could be considered the classic BR fuelling point design is seen at Tinsley in July 1989 with 37068** *Grainflow* **in attendance. The 'v'-shaped roof was the most common configuration on external fuelling points, although the exact design varied, in this case employing corrugated sheet. More unusual were the vertical corrugated plastic screens around the posts and fuel pump that featured on some of the depot's fuelling points.**
Simon Bendall Collection

Fuelling points since privatisation have become much more varied, although those companies that inherited BR facilities have tended to retain them. Thanks to the development of portable storage tanks combined with pumps, fuelling points can now be established with minimal fuss at locations that do not have a high throughput of stock, such as some freight terminals. Various modern offerings are illustrated over the next few pages alongside the different BR types.

Fuelling points

RIGHT: Thornaby was one of the depots to employ pre-cast concrete canopies over its fuelling points, this being a region specific trait that can further help locate a layout in a particular area of the country. As well as the rounded roof, the posts were also concrete, so noticeably thicker than the steel posts found on other regions. 31319 is seen outside the main shed on May 25, 1986.
Simon Bendall Collection

LEFT: Tinsley had six fuelling points installed outside the depot building, three at each end and serving two lines each. 47398 is seen at the north end of the depot in September 1994, the installations on this side lacking the corrugated screens seen in the shot of 37068 at the south end. The Class 47, otherwise known as 47152, carried this revised identity between March 1994 and September 1995 to denote it had been fitted with green circle multiple working equipment. However, once the modification was extended to much of the Railfreight Distribution fleet, the renumbering was reversed.
Simon Bendall Collection

RIGHT: The two fuelling points at Inverness amounted to corrugated lean-to shelters when recorded on July 5, 1984, as 27108 runs past. A concrete apron exists on both sides of the line along with some rubber matting but the track itself is properly sleepered throughout, albeit with ash-style ballast.
Simon Bendall Collection

Modelling BR: Diesel Depots

Fuelling points

RIGHT: A good view of the Longsight fuelling point is afforded during 1990 as 47152 waits to be attended to. The canopy is again corrugated sheet with three strip lights suspended on each edge, while two separate pumps are provided instead of one combined unit. Outside of the covered area, standpipes are provided for a water supply, while the rails are fixed directly to the concrete pad, which is a uniformly oily mess. The adapted garden shed is presumably for storage of supplies. *Simon Bendall Collection*

LEFT: The fuelling point at March was unusual in its design, there being three 'v'-shaped canopies adjacent to each other, these serving just four lines, and all joined above the loco roofs by strengthening girders. Part of this arrangement is seen in 1990 as 47145 *Merddin Emrys* stops by for refuelling. No lights were provided under the canopies, these instead being located on the horizontal bar mid-way up the posts. Above this, vertical corrugated sheets were fitted to a framework with diagonal strengtheners. *Simon Bendall Collection*

RIGHT: A modern interpretation of the classic fuelling point design is seen at Neville Hill, this presumably being roofless due to the proximity of the overhead electrification. Instead, the two posts and crossbeam are there simply for the lighting as 08690 *David Thirkill* stands alongside. The fire extinguisher is now housed in a modern plastic case, although its previous wooden home remains attached to the post alongside. The little kiosk alongside is an interesting addition. Lurking in the background are internal user tank wagons, of which more can be found from page 110. *Simon Bendall Collection*

Fuelling points

LEFT: A modernised fuelling area was provided at St Blazey by EWS, which is seen on June 5, 2001, with 66145 in attendance. This was sited directly alongside the fuel storage tanks and the tanker unloading road with TTA ESSO56006 present. The Cornish depot could manage with just one or two wagons of traction gas oil per week, these being delivered via the Enterprise wagonload service at the time. In 2023, only one depot in the whole of the UK now receives its fuel by rail, this being Neville Hill as a low bridge prevents road tanker access. David Ratcliffe

ABOVE: The former wagon repair and then carriage maintenance depot at Bristol Barton Hill was significantly upgraded by EWS to make it suitable for loco and nowadays unit servicing. As well as building a new maintenance shed, a fuelling point was installed which was a modern take on the BR design. During 2005, the Royal duo of 67005 *Queen's Messenger* and 67006 *Royal Sovereign* repose together. Simon Bendall Collection

ABOVE: Under the ownership of Knights Rail Services and now Arlington Fleet Group, Eastleigh Works has once again become a major centre of rail operations. During 2015, a new high capacity fuelling point was installed to a quite unique design to replace the low-capacity portable tanks previously used. Featuring a horizontal tank, the cabinet on the end contains the hose on a reel along with the pump, gauge, and controls. Seen in August 2023, Colas and GB Railfreight have been particular users of the facility to support their infrastructure operations around the area. Carl Watson

LEFT: What passes for a maintenance facility for DB Cargo on Teesside nowadays is illustrated on May 16, 2023. Following the closure of Thornaby in 2009, a fuelling and light servicing point was created in Tees Yard alongside the traincrew building. A large capacity rectangular fuel tank was also installed alongside, which can just be seen on the left hand edge of the picture. The line on which 66136 is standing also leads to the small wagon repair depot, which was built around the same time, while locos stable on sidings behind the photographer in an otherwise unused part of the yard. Martyn Hilbert

Modelling BR: Diesel Depots **69**

Fuelling points

Fuelling point models

It was not until the early 1990s that a kit for the standard BR fuelling point arrived in OO gauge, courtesy of Knightwing. Up until then, it had been a case of scratchbuild your own, so the plastic offering was something of a game changer and the first batch was eagerly snapped up. Still available today, the kit includes options for both the 'v'-shaped canopy and the rounded style but using the same support posts so is something of a compromise, given the different thicknesses of the concrete and steel posts. It also includes a rectangular base with nice, moulded features, the pump and hoses, and an assortment of other details.

With the gap filled and well at that, it is only in the last decade or so that further options have become available. This is in part due to the rise of decorated and 'ready to plant' structures from the ready to run manufacturers, and the emergence of different styles of refuelling points, allowing further models to be produced. Some of these have been better than others with a selection illustrated below.

ABOVE: Set in the early 1990s when Sectorisation was in full effect, Oulton depicts a busy OO gauge Midlands location with a variety of freight activity, including a cement works and an oil terminal. The work of Allan Cromarty, this view shows a Knightwing fuelling point installed as part of the TMD with an array of colourful locos on shed. Prominent in the line-up is Network SouthEast-liveried 33035 while behind it lurks 47522 *Doncaster Enterprise* in its unique LNER apple green scheme. Also visible are resident pilot 08661 *Europa* in Railfreight Distribution European colours while 20132 can be glimpsed inside the building. Timara Easter

ABOVE: Bachmann has obtained good mileage out of its Scenecraft fuelling point design, which has more than a strong resemblance to Tinsley. First released in 4mm scale, it has subsequently appeared in both 2mm as illustrated and, unusually for the manufacturer, 7mm as well.

ABOVE: More recently, a smaller fuelling point has been added to the Scenecraft range in 4mm, this having echoes of March and a reduced footprint for the space starved layout. A similarly-sized fuelling point with much the same look but for 7mm can be found in the Skytrex range.

ABOVE: A particularly interesting release from Bachmann in 2016 was what is described as a modern servicing point, this being based on the DMU facilities at Exeter, albeit compressed in length. Still measuring 308mm in 4mm scale, it was subsequently produced in both 2mm and 7mm, giving some interesting options for portraying a unit servicing and fuelling point, maybe through the use of low relief.

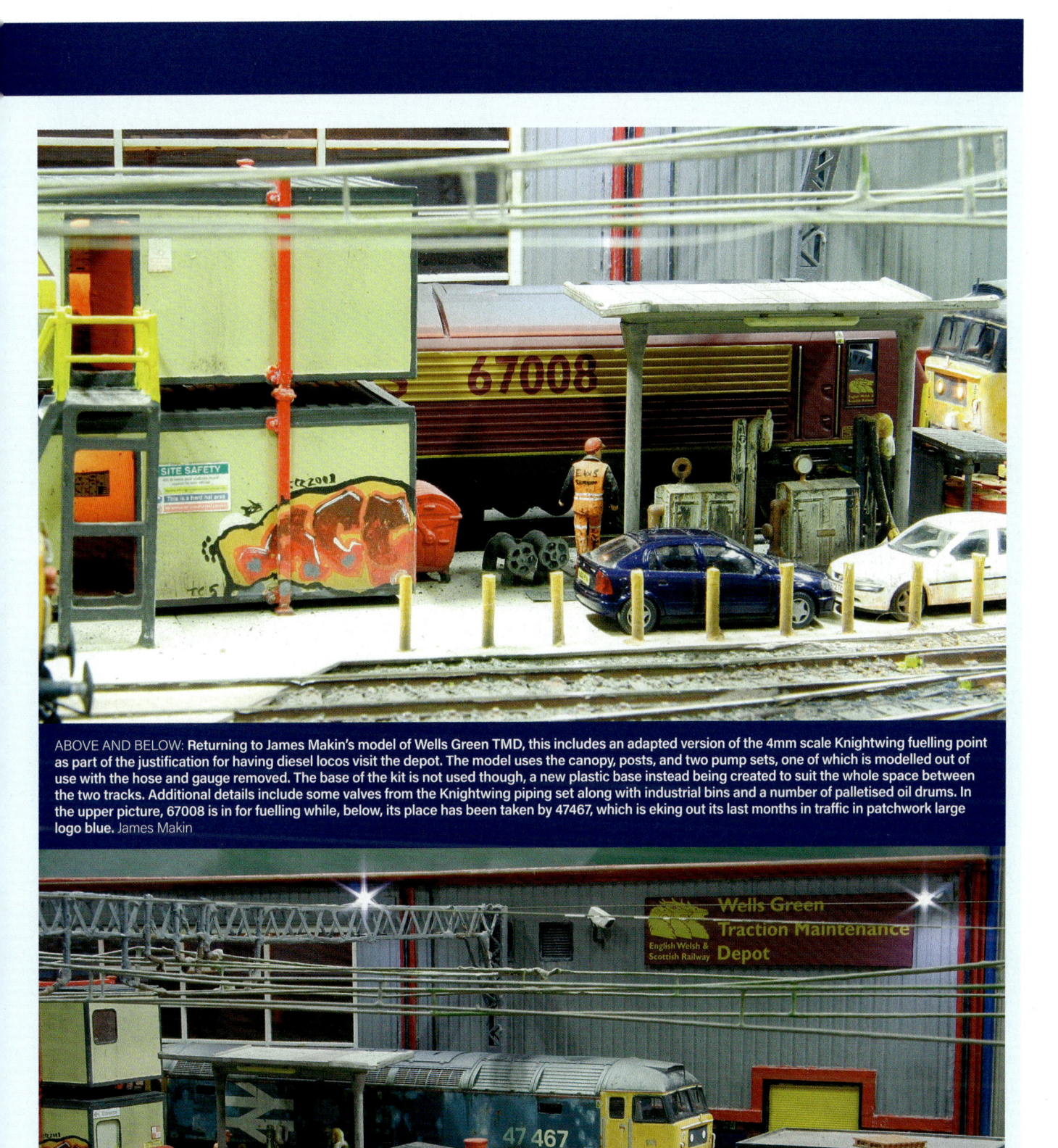

Fuelling points

ABOVE AND BELOW: **Returning to James Makin's model of Wells Green TMD, this includes an adapted version of the 4mm scale Knightwing fuelling point as part of the justification for having diesel locos visit the depot. The model uses the canopy, posts, and two pump sets, one of which is modelled out of use with the hose and gauge removed. The base of the kit is not used though, a new plastic base instead being created to suit the whole space between the two tracks. Additional details include some valves from the Knightwing piping set along with industrial bins and a number of palletised oil drums. In the upper picture, 67008 is in for fuelling while, below, its place has been taken by 47467, which is eking out its last months in traffic in patchwork large logo blue.** James Makin

Modelling BR: Diesel Depots 71

Fuelling points

Fuelling point grids

With most fuelling points having some sort of matting or gridwork between the rails, options were explored as to how best to replicate this. While consideration was given to representing the matting from plasticard, an internet search turned up a simple laser-cut kit from Railway Laser Lines to represent the grid style instead. One was duly purchased for evaluation and happy with the results, a few more followed.

Two versions are produced in 4mm scale to suit the sleeper spacing of either Peco Code 75/100 track or the more recent Code 75 bullhead system with its improved appearance. In addition, a 7mm version is also available. The grids can either be supplied as just the centre section to go in the four foot or with narrower outer pieces that sit over the ends of the sleepers on both sides.

The central section of grid has two side pieces to support it on top of the sleepers, these sliding into pre-cut slots which are notched along the lower edge to fit over the sleepers. Assembly is straightforward with glue applied to the slots and the sides then pushed into place. This is best done with the centre section supported on a strip of wood since the parts are quite fragile, while Deluxe Materials Glue 'n' Glaze was used as the adhesive since it dries quickly and clear.

The side sections also have two supports with the narrower one fitting into slots along the centreline of the grid while the wider piece goes into notches down the side. As the side sections are a bit fiddlier to assemble due to their narrower size, the gluing was done on a piece of plastic laminate-faced board to prevent the glue from sticking everything to a wooden surface. A piece of square section steel was also used to hold things in place until the glue dried.

Since these grids were going over wider P4 gauge track, it was decided to bulk out the sides of the assembled centre sections to compensate for the larger gap between the rails. This was achieved by gluing lengths of 40 thou by 20 thou styrene strip to both sides. Once everything was dry, the parts were painted using an airbrush and Humbrol No.85 satin black to give the glossy sheen often found around fuelling points.

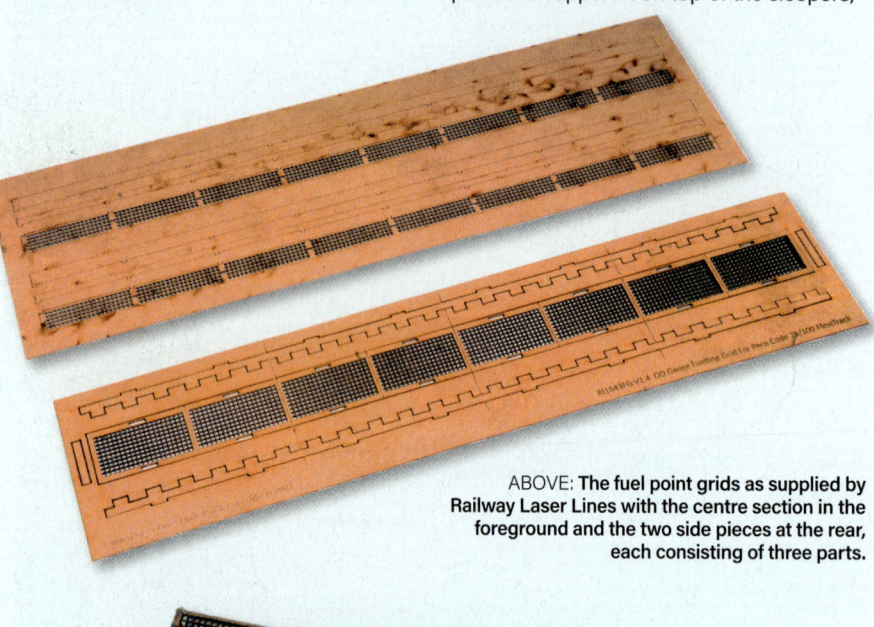

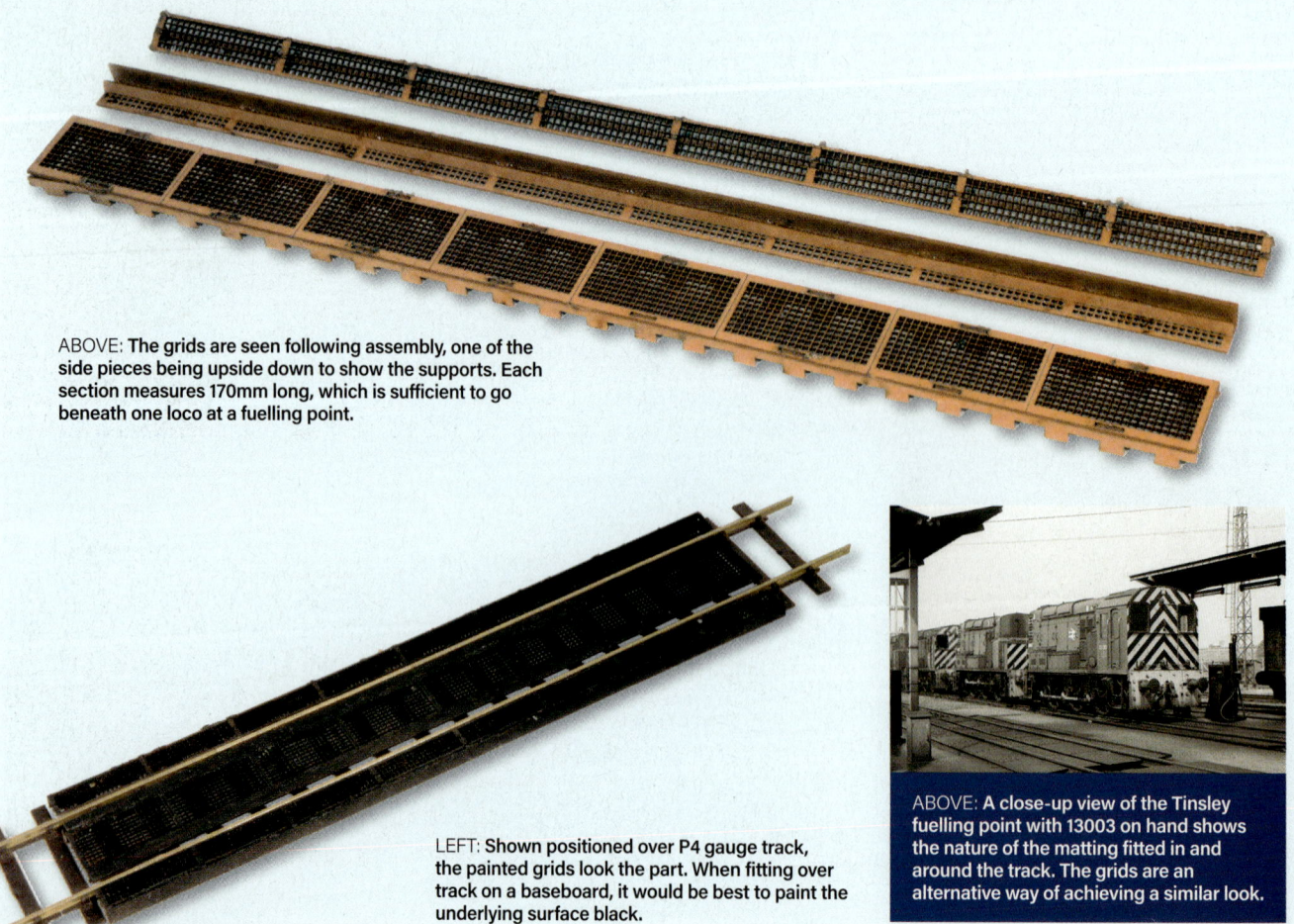

ABOVE: The fuel point grids as supplied by Railway Laser Lines with the centre section in the foreground and the two side pieces at the rear, each consisting of three parts.

ABOVE: The grids are seen following assembly, one of the side pieces being upside down to show the supports. Each section measures 170mm long, which is sufficient to go beneath one loco at a fuelling point.

LEFT: Shown positioned over P4 gauge track, the painted grids look the part. When fitting over track on a baseboard, it would be best to paint the underlying surface black.

ABOVE: A close-up view of the Tinsley fuelling point with 13003 on hand shows the nature of the matting fitted in and around the track. The grids are an alternative way of achieving a similar look.

Fuelling points

A portable fuelling point

For low use situations, a portable style of fuel installation is available at some locations, such as freight terminals for diesel shunters. Two such examples were recorded at Eastleigh Works during 2011, these being placed close to each other but some way from the workshop buildings.

These consist of an outer plastic shell with internal fuel tank, pump, hose, and fuel nozzle to give a self-contained unit, although an electrical supply is required to power the pump. As the photos show, the ubiquitous fire extinguisher in a plastic case is never far away along with a bin for waste.

A 3D print of a slightly different design to that pictured is produced in both 2mm and 4mm by Rusty Rails Modelling, these being supplied as a triple pack and as a pair respectively. These are one-piece prints, just requiring painting to finish. If desired, further detailing could be added such as the hose and accessories.

LEFT: One of the portable fuel pumps seen at Eastleigh from the front with the power cable, which is buried in the ballast, running from ground level to the socket on the left of the hatch.

ABOVE: A close-up of the hatch with the nozzle to the right.

ABOVE: One of the prints following painting, Humbrol No. 117 being employed in this instance.

ABOVE: The second portable installation at Eastleigh is seen from the rear with fire extinguisher and bin in attendance. The obligatory health and safety notice has faded somewhat in the sun. Behind stands 73119 *Borough of Eastleigh* and Mk.2d BFK 17159 then in DRS ownership.

RIGHT: The pair of 4mm scale 3D prints as supplied by Rusty Rails Modelling.

Modelling BR: Diesel Depots

Fuelling points

Where 'Westerns' and Class 50s once filled the shed with noise and fumes, Fertis-liveried Class 56s sit in silence in the servicing shed at Old Oak Common on March 28, 2009, awaiting the next chapter of their careers. Happily, both 56051 and 56113 found a new operator in Colas Rail while 08879 also still exists but only in store. The fuelling equipment remained operational and in use pretty much to the depot's demise. Simon Bendall

Fuelling sheds

To supplement the images of fuelling points, **Simon Bendall** presents a selection of views of fuelling sheds across the decades, these featuring the pump equipment in covered accommodation.

LEFT: Along the Great Western Main Line at Bristol Bath Road, three 'Peaks' stand inside the fuelling shed in the late 1970s. While all are unidentified, it provides a comparison of front end styles with the centre box and split box locos soon to rebuilt with marker lights like their sister in the middle road. This was the depot building nearest to the platforms at Temple Meads and would be extended by roughly a loco length in 1982, the new section not matching what was already there. Simon Bendall Collection

RIGHT: Tinsley-allocated 47307 *Bunting* was a long way from home at it shunts around Eastfield depot in 1989 in the company of 20185 and 20199. Immediately above the Class 20s is the fuelling shelter while the fuel storage tanks, and pump house are also on show. Simon Bendall Collection

74 www.keymodelworld.com

Fuelling points

ABOVE: Class 56s were once strangers to Scotland but by the early 1990s were increasingly used on Anglo-Scottish coal workings. The long distance journeys were fuel intensive with Trainload Coal-branded 56129 being topped up at Ayr TMD on May 30, 1994; the loco now being a Trainload Freight West (later Transrail) asset. Simon Bendall Collection

ABOVE: As a primarily electric railway, the erstwhile Southern Region was not overly populated with diesel maintenance facilities. However, Hither Green was still functioning into the EWS era as 73133 *The Bluebell Railway* shows off its thankfully unique route learning modifications inside the fuelling shed in 1998. Simon Bendall Collection

RIGHT: The walls of the former steam shed at Exeter depot have been put to good use to provide some measure of covered accommodation over the fuelling point as a thirsty 33114 is re-fuelled on April 2, 1992, having stood in for the booked Class 47/7 on a Waterloo-Exeter working. Simon Bendall Collection

BELOW: With the closure of Immingham TMD, a new fuelling facility was constructed by DB Cargo a short distance away in the sorting sidings. Commissioned in November 2020, 66176 makes a pit-stop under the boldly-finished structure on August 9, 2022. Similar in style to the Gresty Bridge fuelling shed seen overleaf, this would make an interesting model, one that would not fade to pink like this inevitably will! Craig Adamson

Modelling BR: Diesel Depots 75

Fuelling points

LEFT: The Gresty Bridge fuelling point is seen in its current form in March 2014 with the blue-painted shelter in place alongside the pre-existing brick building. The taller stores building behind was constructed after the fuelling shelter had been put in place. Long enough to accommodate one loco, it is a dead end road with the bufferstop obscured by 57302 *Chad Varah* with 47805 *John Scott 12.5.45-22.5.12* alongside. Both locos are now with Locomotive Services.
Simon Bendall

Gresty Bridge in focus

DRS' Crewe depot has changed substantially over the years, works have included building a shed extension, a revamped fuelling point and a new stores building. **Simon Bendall** takes a closer look at the enhanced fuelling facilities.

ABOVE: Back in July 2008, the Gresty Bridge fuelling point looked very different, it still being largely as inherited when DRS brought the depot to expand its maintenance facilities. A tank on a brick bund is surrounded by supplementary tanks and the pump.

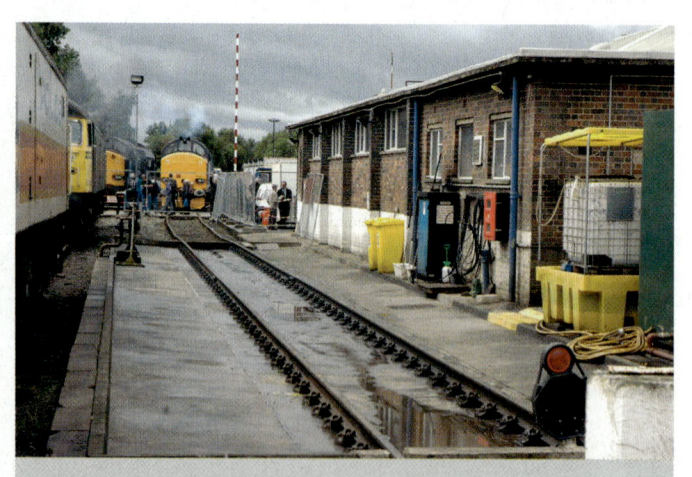

ABOVE: A look at the concrete apron around the fuelling road shows the outer sections are sloped so spillages drain towards the centre of the track. Kerb stones are also provided all the way round. This apron remains in place today beneath the blue shelter.

ABOVE: By the time of the next DRS open day at Crewe two years later, much of the equipment had been replaced by a new high capacity fuel tank with integrated pump equipment housed in the cabinet. On top, a walkway was provided around an inspection hatch.

ABOVE: Seen from the other side, the new fuel tank includes lifting eyes along the top edge to allow it to be craned into position. The three intermediate bulk containers (IBC) sitting on spill bunds each contain different types of cleaning fluid, including 'Trainsheen'.

Fuelling points

RIGHT: **Looking down the fuelling shelter during the August 2012 open day shows the cut-out on the right hand side to accommodate the pump cabinet on the fuel tank. Railway Laser Lines offers an impressive-looking laser-cut kit for the shelter in both 4mm and 7mm, with a shorter version also available in the senior scale.** Simon Bendall

Gresty Bridge fuel tank by Terry Bendall

This fuel tank is heavily based on the one at Gresty Bridge and was entirely scratchbuilt in 4mm. The basis of the model was a block of wood cut and planed to the correct size with a smaller piece of wood glued to one side to form the core of the pump cabinet. The block was then clad with separate rectangles of 40 thou styrene to represent the various panels welded together on the prototype, care being taken to ensure that these fitted tightly together. The styrene panels were fixed to the wood using a thin layer of impact adhesive.

The same method was employed for the cabinet with two pieces of 10 thou styrene glued to the front to make the doors. The hinges were represented with small slivers of five thou styrene, while a door handle was formed using 0.3mm brass wire bent to shape and glued into holes made in the door.

The walkway was formed from brass with a piece of suitable mesh used for the base with 1mm square base soldered all round. The guard rail was made from 1mm brass angle with holes drilled to take 0.45mm brass wire for the railings. To assemble these, the corner posts were soldered into place on the base and the wire threaded through and soldered, after which the projecting ends were cut off and filed smooth on the outside. The ladder came from a section of signal ladder etch sourced from Wizard Models. Underneath the tank, the supports were cut from brass channel section and glued in place, while the lifting eyes were formed using brass from a piece of scrap etch.

The main part of the tank was painted using an airbrush with Humbrol No.25 employed for the dark blue and No.64 for the ladder and platform. After painting, a thin wash of Railmatch sleeper grime was applied to tone things down.

The intermediate bulk container on a spill bund is available in 4mm from 3D Printed

ABOVE: **The Gresty Bridge tank employs styrene cladding over a wooden core, with the walkway being scratchbuilt from brass.**

Corner, this coming as a three-piece unpainted print. This was painted as per the ones at Gresty Bridge with Humbrol No.24 used for the yellow base and No.11 silver for the frame. The tank was initially painted white (No.34) to represent the clear plastic. Once this was dry, much of the tank was then over-painted with Humbrol No.94 brown-yellow to represent liquid inside.

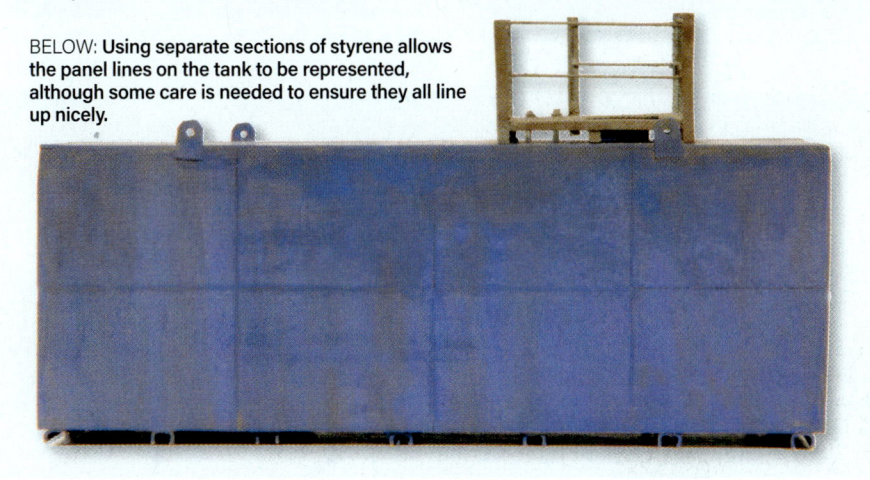

BELOW: **Using separate sections of styrene allows the panel lines on the tank to be represented, although some care is needed to ensure they all line up nicely.**

ABOVE LEFT: **The model of the IBC and bund as supplied by 3D Printed Corner, the tank pushing out from its support frame to ease painting.**

ABOVE RIGHT: **Liquid in the container can be represented using paint, in this case a yellow-brown shade from Humbrol.**

Modelling BR: Diesel Depots 77

Fuelling points

Depot fuel tanks

With fuelling points and sheds came the need to store large quantities of fuel on depots, bringing the construction of storage tanks that were as diverse as everything else. Simon Bendall looks at some examples.

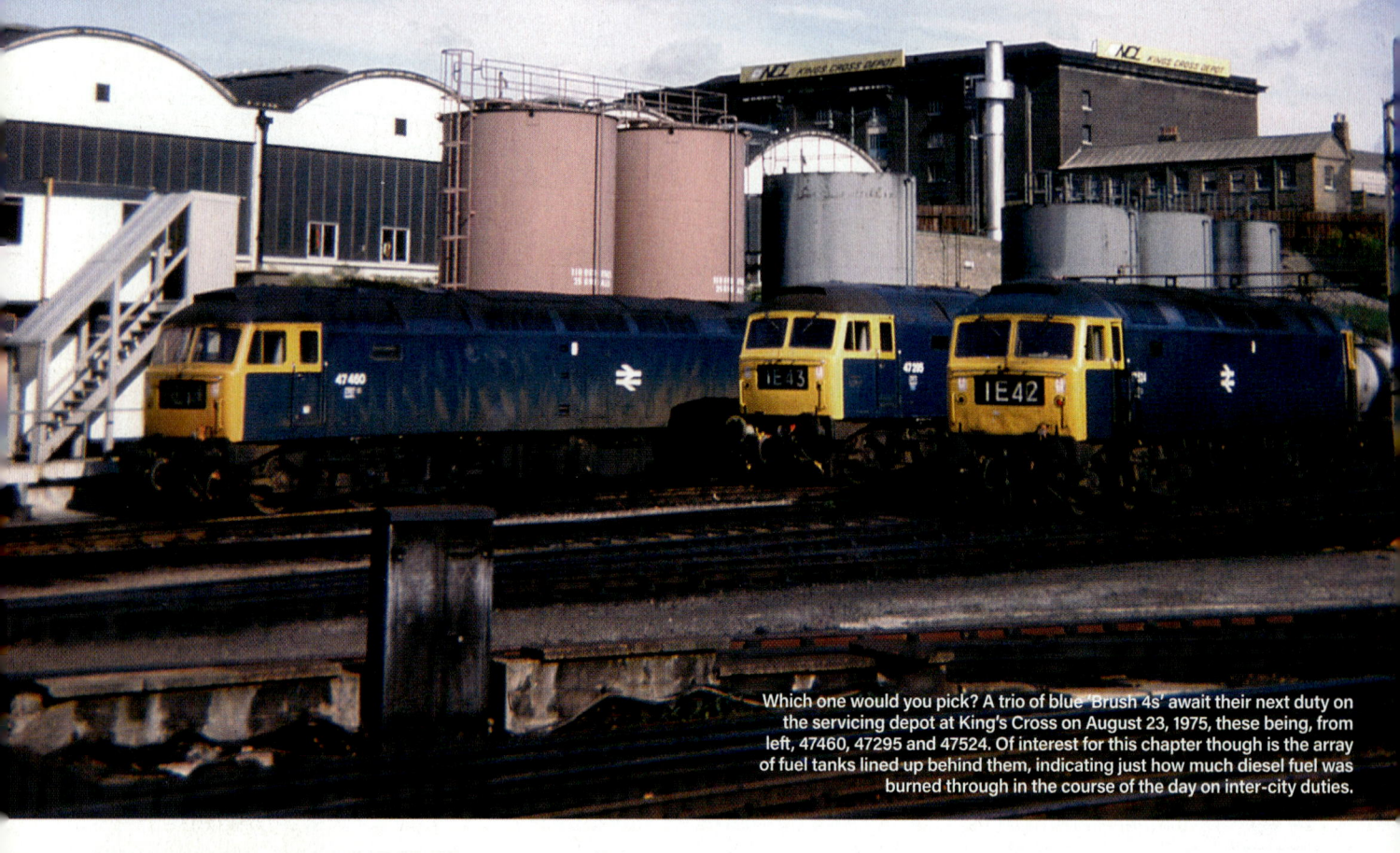

Which one would you pick? A trio of blue 'Brush 4s' await their next duty on the servicing depot at King's Cross on August 23, 1975, these being, from left, 47460, 47295 and 47524. Of interest for this chapter though is the array of fuel tanks lined up behind them, indicating just how much diesel fuel was burned through in the course of the day on inter-city duties.

The introduction of diesel traction brought a new logistical challenge for British Railways as it was now faced with having to deliver thousands of gallons of traction gas oil to depots across the country on a regular basis, with all the inherent dangers of moving such quantities of highly flammable liquid around. While coal may have been messy and labour intensive, at least it wasn't generally explosive!

The answer lay in constructing storage tanks at the depots so at least a stock could be maintained on site, which could then be regularly replenished without creating a gap in supply. Tanks were not the only infrastructure required though as space needed to be found for tank wagons to be discharged and a pump house installed to distribute the fuel. While having the fuelling points located near the storage tanks was the ideal solution, this was not always possible due to the depot layouts, so the fuel would have to be pumped across the depot, either underground or via high level pipes.

The size and number of storage tanks provided varied depending on the requirements of each depot; unsurprisingly, those facilities with large and busy allocations could be expected to have greater storage capacity than a depot on a secondary route. Space was also an issue as some depots could not accommodate large diameter tanks so, for example, would have two smaller ones instead to compensate.

Some depots did without tall vertical tanks altogether, instead receiving smaller horizontal ones, the number provided sometimes having to be higher to give the necessary capacity. The tanks, be they vertical or horizontal, would be installed inside a brick or concrete bund to retain any leakage, with a maze of pipework radiating out along with isolating valves and the like. Inspection ladders, stairs and walkways would also be a feature depending on the tank style.

RIGHT: A line of five Esso TTAs, led by ESSO56269, await unloading at Plymouth Laira in November 1991, having recently arrived from Fawley refinery with traction gas oil. For many years, Esso was a major supplier of TGO, not only from its refineries at Fawley and Herbrandston but also from the inland distribution depots at Bromford Bridge and Colwick. As a result, the unbranded grey TTAs were a familiar sight at depots across the country. Mark Saunders

Fuelling points

At Cambridge, the fuel tank siding, storage tanks and fuelling point were all in close proximity, but this was a rarity. 08539 stands atop two Shell TTAs during 1991, the slip alongside adding some complexity to the depot's trackwork. Simon Bendall Collection

RIGHT: Squeezed between the running lines and an embankment, the two storage tanks at Leicester needed to be narrower in diameter as a consequence. 47224 stands alongside on May 1, 1990. The red oxide colour was common for the tanks, be they vertical or horizontal, and indeed can still be seen on the Toton examples today. Simon Bendall Collection

BELOW: Bescot TMD is nowadays a shadow of its former self and largely retained for wagon maintenance. Seen from above, the modern two-road 'tin shed' occupies the site of the former TMD building, while the area at the bottom of the picture is the site of the former steam shed. What does still survive though is the array of storage tanks, nine in total, and the pump house. Several London Midland depots had this style of storage tank arrangement but with less tanks, including Allerton and Buxton. 66117 departs the yard on August 14, 2021, with the 4E94 Southampton-Rotherham Masborough intermodal. Rob Higgins

Modelling BR: Diesel Depots 79

Fuelling points

LEFT: **At Old Oak Common, a single large diameter storage tank was provided alongside the Factory and with an access road running to it by the boundary fence. When recorded in August 2008, the lack of maintenance had allowed the bund to become overgrown and it was also full of water, proving that at least it didn't leak!**
Simon Bendall

ABOVE: **The long disused tanker road at Old Oak Common with the discharge pipe and valves still in situ. The depot's fuel had arrived by road for a number of years.**

ABOVE: **The now derelict pump room was directly alongside the storage tank with a mass of pipework running between the two and the discharge valves.**

ABOVE: **A closer look at the forest of pipes and valves outside the pump room.**

ABOVE: **By this time, the steps over the bund were of more use as a diving board!**

Fuelling points

LEFT: The completed fuel storage tanks along with the pump house are seen on their sub-base ready for installation on the layout. This uses plastic tank kits from Kibri and a laser-cut pump house from Railway Laser Lines.

Modelling depot tanks

Various options exist to portray depot fuel storage tanks, encompassing both ready to plant structures and kits. Terry Bendall takes two of the latter to create a depot scene inspired by Old Oak Common.

You can spend quite some time searching the internet for models of fuel storage tanks to suit 4mm scale, there being a number of options. Taking HO scale offerings into account as well, some are far too toylike, while others are too large, being intended for models of oil refineries.

After a lengthy and at times frustrating search, the Kibri range finally turned up a suitable tank that would fit the space available and compared well to photos of those at TMDs. Although in HO, the size meant that the scale difference between 3.5mm and 4mm would not be readily apparent. However, with no UK retailer having stock of the MIRO deep tank (reference no.39830), two kits were instead sourced from a German supplier and arrived without fuss.

As supplied, each tank consists of three identical rings, the top of the tank, spiral stairs, an assortment of pipes and fittings, and a concrete-style bund with sloping walls. The latter was immediately discarded as it was not suitable for a TMD, but the rest of the contents was largely employed as intended, except for some of the smaller details. Assembled as per the instructions, the two tanks went together well and were later sprayed with an airbrush using Humbrol No.64. When this was dry, they were weathered using a wash of Railmatch sleeper grime.

Forming a bund

Work on creating a replacement brick-built bund wall began by cutting a piece of 20 thou styrene to form a base. The dimensions

ABOVE: The Kibri tank kit following the assembly of the main components, which are the three tank rings, base, and the top. To this have been added the spiral steps and top rail. Ideally, the railing should be taller for use on a TMD and may well be changed for one scratchbuilt from brass wire later.

ABOVE: The completed bund following construction from styrene sheet and embossed brick plasticard. This has been painted, the mortar wash added, and the base given an initial coat of stone colour to act as an undercoat for later weathering.

Modelling BR: Diesel Depots **81**

Fuelling points

for this were first worked out by putting the two tanks in the planned position and adding a bit of extra space for the pipework and other fittings. The walls were made by cutting strips of 40 thou styrene, which were then clad on one side with Slaters brick embossed sheet. Once glued in place on the base, further strips of brick effect sheet were glued to the outside faces, taking care to try and maintain the bonding of the brickwork. The last stage was to glue thin strips of brick sheet to the tops of the walls.

The base was next painted by hand using Humbrol No.121 pale stone which is a reasonable match for concrete. When the base colour was dry, the same paint was applied to the brick walls and then almost immediately wiped off again. This leaves some of the stone colour in the embossed mortar course of the brickwork. When everything was dry, a fairly heavy coat of dark grey was applied as a wash to represent grime encrusted brickwork and concrete.

Pump it up

The pump house is a Railway Laser Lines kit and based on the one at Cardiff Canton, the kit also being available in O gauge. The company also offers a similarly nice model of a larger fuel line and maintenance office based on the one by the Toton fuelling point.

The Canton-inspired kit consists of a laser-cut internal shell along with outer walls with a brick effect cut into them to clad it. Also included are door and window parts and components for the roof. The kit was again assembled as per the instructions with the inner shell consisting of four walls, the floor and roof. This all slots together using the laser cut joints with PVA woodworking glue used as the adhesive.

Once dry, the wall cladding was fitted into place. These have the corners notched to

ABOVE: **The first stage of putting together the pump house is to glue together the floor and four inner wall sections.**

ABOVE: **The next stage is to add the brick cladding sheets, ensuring a good fit on the corners. In this view, initial painting has begun with the walls finished in red oxide and the interior given a coat of white. The door is also in place but not yet painted.**

ABOVE: **The components of the Railway Laser Lines kit for the Cardiff Canton pump house as supplied.**

82 www.keymodelworld.com

Fuelling points

continue the bonding of the brickwork and, while they fit tightly together, it is important to do a dry fit all the way round to ensure everything lines up. If any gaps do occur on the joints, these can be easily filled afterwards.

The instructions suggest painting the walls using a red oxide cellulose primer with a grey version for the roof parts. This worked well and the red oxide gives a good base colour for the brickwork. After the paint was dry, a thin wash of Humbrol stone colour (No.121) was once again applied and wiped off to represent the mortar. This toned down the red colour of the brickwork, which was then weathered with a wash of dark brown to darken things further.

The door and windows were then fitted, a process that needed a bit of filing to get everything to fit nicely, while the windows were then glazed using 20 thou thick clear styrene. A nice touch with the kit is the separate laser-cut door frame, which can be painted off the model, thereby ensuring a much neater finish that trying to paint it as part of the door. The frame was then glued in place using Deluxe Materials Glue 'n' Glaze which I find very useful for this sort of job as it dries clear and can be scraped off when dry if it gets in the wrong place.

The instructions suggest gluing a thin layer of sand to the roof to represent a felt roof with gravel finish. Feeling this would be a bit overscale, a piece of 400 grit abrasive paper was employed instead, which seems to work well and is easier to apply.

Installation

With the tanks, bund and pump house all finished, they were all glued in position on a sub-base, this being made from 40 thou black styrene and profiled to fit the space available on the baseboard. This allows the final detailing work to be carried out in comfort at the workbench, rather than leaning over the baseboard.

A lot of time was spent studying photos of Old Oak Common and other tank installations to get an impression of the mass of pipework and working out how best to represent it. Much of the pipework and fittings supplied with the Kibri kits were employed, along with various parts from the scrapbox, such as Knightwing pipes, allowing a reasonable representation to be created. Fixing the various parts in place was a bit time consuming and it was often necessary to use bits of wood and styrene off-cuts to support things while the glue dried. Finally, the steps over the wall of the bund that came with the tank kit were painted and put in place as a finishing touch.

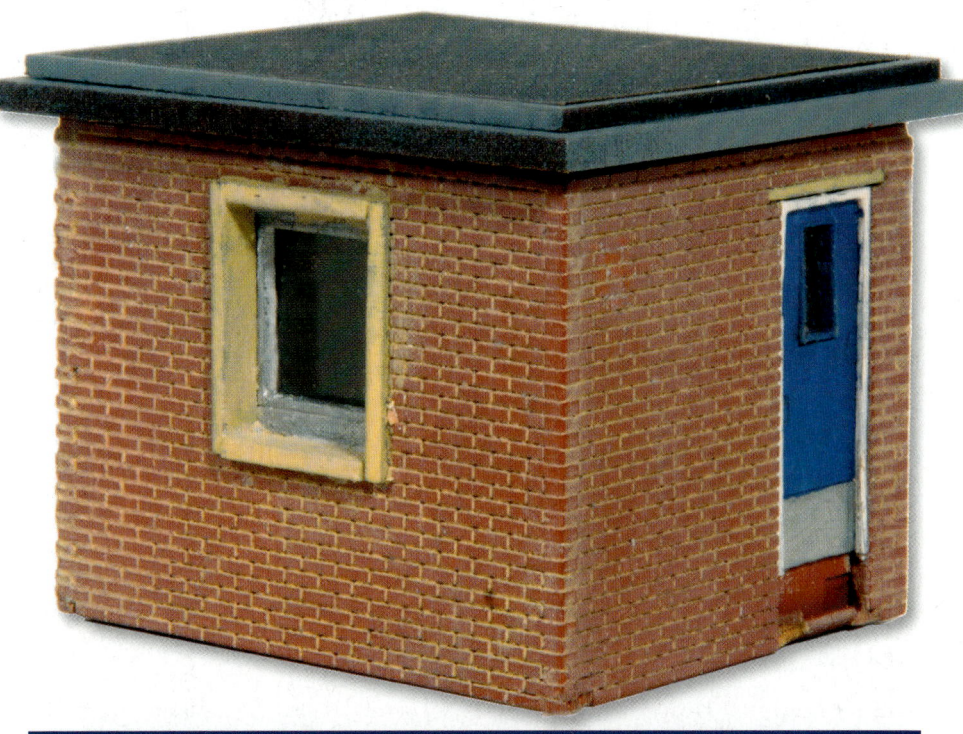

ABOVE: **The finished pump house with the roof glued in place. A step is required beneath the door, which was added following gluing to the sub-base.**

ABOVE: **With the mortar wash added, the detail painting can be carried out, such as the door and window frames, before fitting the glazing in the windows. Adding some abrasive paper to the roof gives a felt effect and does not require painting.**

Modelling BR: Diesel Depots **83**

Fuelling points

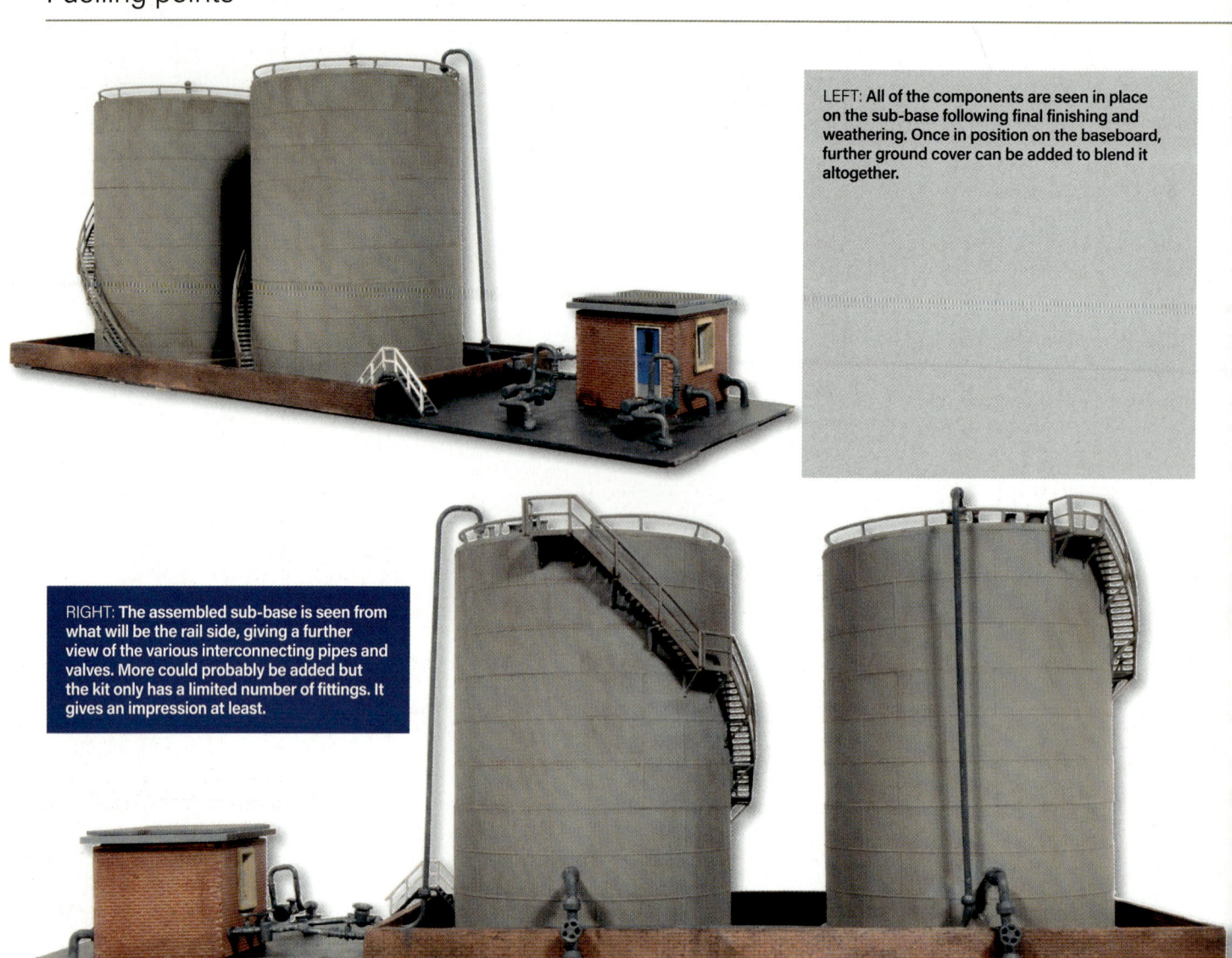

LEFT: All of the components are seen in place on the sub-base following final finishing and weathering. Once in position on the baseboard, further ground cover can be added to blend it altogether.

RIGHT: The assembled sub-base is seen from what will be the rail side, giving a further view of the various interconnecting pipes and valves. More could probably be added but the kit only has a limited number of fittings. It gives an impression at least.

ABOVE: Virtually all of the components of a depot's fuelling system are seen in this view of Toton on September 22, 1984, with 31118 and a 'Peak' in view. Towering above everything though is the depot's water tank. John Dedman

KEY MODEL WORLD MODEL SHOP

Limited editions • Exclusive products • Modelling essentials

IN STOCK NOW!

AVAILABLE NOW! Exclusive laser-cut diesel depot kits for 'OO'

Available now from the Key Model World Shop are exclusive laser-cut diesel depot kits for 'OO' gauge. Based on Stratford in East London, the kits are available in two forms: a four-road through shed measuring 367mm x 312mm and a four-road shed with an office at the rear and stores to one side measuring 427mm x 410mm.

£85.00 Option A

£135.00 Option B

Available now exclusively from the Key Model World Shop.

SCAN THE QR CODE TO VIEW OUR FULL RANGE OF EXCLUSIVE LASER-CUT AND 3D PRINTED MODELLING KITS ONLINE

Scan the QR code for full details of all our modelling products or visit...

www.keymodelworld.com/shop

Ancillary structures

Ancillary structures

While maintenance and fuelling facilities were the most important aspects of a depot, there were a number of other buildings that would contribute towards its function. Simon Bendall **takes a look at a selection of these secondary and sometimes over-looked structures.**

An army marches on its stomach and so it could be said does a railway workforce. A depot could have all the repair facilities possible, but they would count for nothing without some staff amenities. This along with other secondary structures can sometimes be overlooked on a layout in the eagerness to fit in another stabling road or find somewhere for those lifting jacks to go.

In the same vein, it can be asked 'where do all the spare parts for repairing those locos live'? Or 'where does the depot admin take place'? Thinking about such matters when planning a layout and leaving sufficient room for the less glamorous aspects can result in a model that is much more realistic if that is your goal. The following chapter once again provides some pictorial inspiration as to what could be portrayed as well as showing how to model a few of them.

ABOVE: The early 1980s saw a steam-cleaning facility constructed at Old Oak Common, where locos and DMU cars could be cleaned prior to maintenance, this particularly relating to the underframes to remove oil, dirt, and grease. In addition, high level walkways were installed for roof cleaning, but these incurred the ire of the unions, who were unhappy that they posed a risk to anyone leaning out of a cab during shunting. As a result, the facility was eventually black-listed and fell into disuse, earning the nickname the 'elephant house' as in the home of white elephants. In later years, it was used as a maintenance base by the Fifty Fund and survived to the end of the West London depot, being pictured on August 30, 2008. Simon Bendall

RIGHT: Although Bristol Barton Hill underwent considerable modernisation in the early years of EWS, this narrow block, complete with fragile roof warning, provided some staff facilities and was sited near the depot throat. With the modern maintenance building out of shot to the right, it provides an interesting comparison between old and new features that was common at depots as they underwent piecemeal upgrades. The block was later demolished with the plot now largely empty except for some relay cabinets. Sometime in 2000, 08896 *Stephen Dent* **is captured at rest between duties.** Simon Bendall Collection

Ancillary structures

ABOVE: **Although its original use is unknown, this small building at Crewe Gresty Bridge is typical of the sort of redundant structure that could be found littering many a depot. Located near to the front of the shed building, it was recorded in October 2012 but later demolished. Next to it is a storage cage for gas bottles, DRS following good practice in storing these away from the depot. Numerous pallets of new brake blocks are also evident as are two sets of miniature snowploughs, these being labelled up as in good condition and suitable for re-use. In the background are the scrap metals skips that all good depots should have.** Simon Bendall

ABOVE: **By November 2008, the traincrew mess building at Old Oak Common was out of use and the doors blocked off with sleepers and junk to stop unauthorised access. Adjoining it is the administration block, which was still seeing some use by the skeleton staff on site at weekends.** Simon Bendall

ABOVE: **A two-storey staff block adjoined Healey Mills depot, which is seen in April 2008, almost two years after the depot closed for good, The rundown of the Yorkshire facility by EWS was protracted, it remained open as a traincrew depot to facilitate crew changes on passing freights for some years after locomotive maintenance had ceased.** Simon Bendall

ABOVE: **Returning to Old Oak Common, the rear of the stores building is seen in August 2008, it was still in use but with items progressively seeing removal by road, doubtless to Toton. Out of shot to the right is the servicing depot with the Factory to the left, a wooden shelter being provided over the walking route between the two. In front of this, the single storey building features security grilles over the windows as trespass was a regular occurrence.** Simon Bendall

RIGHT: **The most modern building at Old Oak Common was this prefabricated structure containing offices for engineering staff and two classrooms. Seen in December 2008, the presence of 56113 gives its location away as by the turntable and next to the servicing shed. With the original Great Western building behind, structures from three different eras were within feet of each other.** Simon Bendall

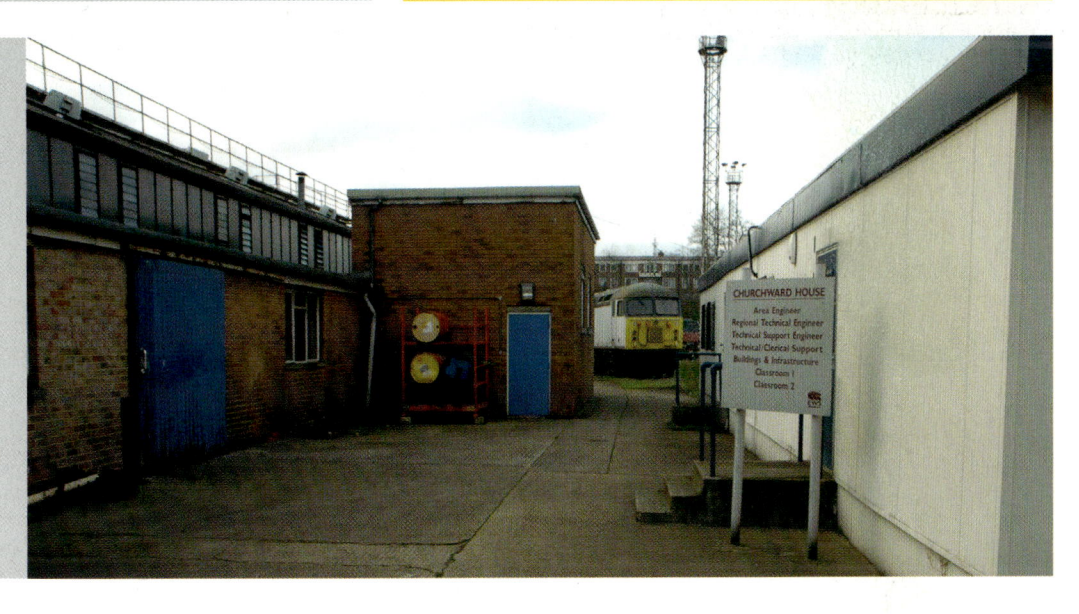

Modelling BR: Diesel Depots

Ancillary structures

Scratchbuilding a staff block by Terry Bendall

ABOVE: The finished staff block seen from the mess room end, with the lobby in the centre and toilet/wash block at the far end, the latter being windowless on this side as it will be next to the depot wall.

The inspiration for this staff block came from the building that still stands at Leicester depot, although it was not a direct copy. A number of photos were to hand, although none were close-up, but these were sufficient to estimate the size of the building, which had to be adapted anyway to suit the space. The Leicester building clearly consisted of separate parts, including a lobby, staff mess, and toilet/wash block so this layout was adopted. It also meant the model could be built as three separate units and joined together at the end of the build.

Previous experience had shown that for small buildings of this nature, a single thickness of brick embossed styrene sheet reinforced with strips of styrene on the inside was sufficient to give a rigid structure. The walls were marked out and openings for doors and windows cut using a fine scalpel blade. The window openings were made 1mm larger all round to allow for a piece of 40 thou styrene strip to be glued round the edges to represent the concrete window surrounds. Additional strips of 40 thou styrene were glued to the corners of each building side to enable a strong joint to be created and yet more similar strips were cut to fit between the window openings to provide a recess where the glazing would later be fitted. These also help to strengthens the walls.

Basic assembly

Once all the walls had been completed, they were joined together using liquid polystyrene cement as the adhesive. Care needs to be taken to ensure that the walls are joined at right angles and a useful aid to doing this are corner clamps. I have some picked up years ago at an exhibition which will hold two walls at right angles, although I have not found the same product since.

ABOVE: The central lobby section of the building is seen with its four walls glued together, while the styrene sheet inserted at the top of the walls to keep things square can also be glimpsed.

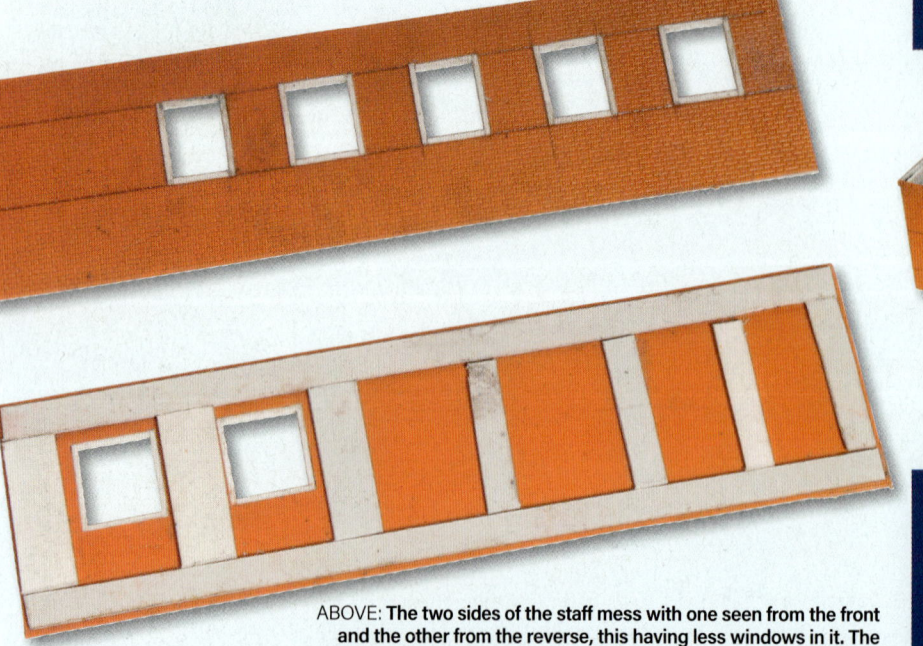

ABOVE: The two sides of the staff mess with one seen from the front and the other from the reverse, this having less windows in it. The method of adding 40 thou styrene strips to strengthen the brick sheet can be seen in addition to the strips lining the window apertures.

ABOVE: The lobby is seen again but from the rear, showing how the recessed doorway is made from styrene. The strengthening piece to fit around the top of the walls lies alongside with the roof next to it. The latter has a square of styrene underneath that matches the aperture in the strengthener, allowing it to notch in place.

Ancillary structures

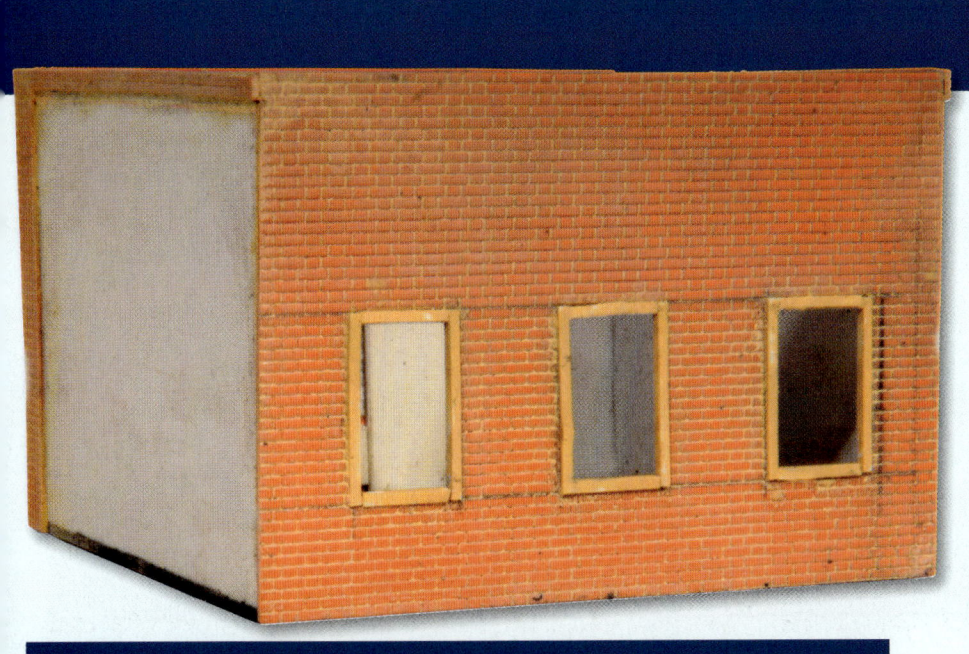

ABOVE: The walls of one section are seen following the application of the mortar wash all over, while the window frames have also been painted in the same colour. The bare plastic wall will adjoin one of the other building sections so lacks any cosmetic detail.

The best way to assemble each set of four walls is to clamp them in two pairs and when the glue has set, then join the two pairs to make the basic structure. Before joining the walls though, a piece of 40 thou styrene was cut to form a floor and inserting this in place, without any glue, while the wall joints are drying helps to keep the structure square.

With the walls dried, a similar piece of styrene was cut to fit between the tops of the walls, which also helps to keep things square. This had a rectangular hole cut in the middle which helps to locate the roof in the correct position and also gives access so an interior and lighting can be added if desired. For example, 3D Printing Corner does kitchen equipment, worktops, tables, plastic chairs, and other useful bits to fit out a mess room interior.

Adding the roof

The roof was also made in three separate sections to mirror the three parts of the building, the one over the lobby being slightly pitched with the other two completely flat. The underside of each roof had a flat base, which included an additional piece of styrene to locate in the hole mentioned above. An edging strip of styrene measuring 5mm by 1mm was glued around the underneath of the roof sections to represent the large soffits on the prototype building, these also concealing any gaps between the underside of the roof and the walls!

Painting of the outside of the walls was done at this stage using a Humbrol brick red, after which a fairly thick wash of Humbrol No. 121 stone colour was applied all over and then wiped off to leave a residue in the mortar joints. When this was dry, small amounts of a range of suitable colours were put on a palette and individual bricks picked out to give a range of tones. Once this was done, a thin wash of brown was applied to blend everything together and mute the colours.

Final finishing

The next stage was to fit the glazing. To do this, pieces of 20 thou thick clear styrene were cut to fit the recesses on the inside of the walls. These were then held in place while the outline of the window opening was traced round using the point of a scalpel. The piece of clear styrene was then put on a cutting mat and a line scribed round 0.5mm inside the previously traced line.

Strips were then cut from a self-adhesive address label and stuck onto the glazing to represent the window frame, including bars to represent opening windows. This method saves having to cut and paint plastic strips to make the frames and avoids the risk of getting glue on the glazing. The finished windows were then fixed in place using Deluxe Materials' Glue 'n' Glaze.

On the roofs, each section was covered with abrasive paper cut to size and glued in place, this representing the felt coverings often found on flat and shallow roofs. With all three sections completed, they were then joined together to form one building and any final fettling to the joints carried out.

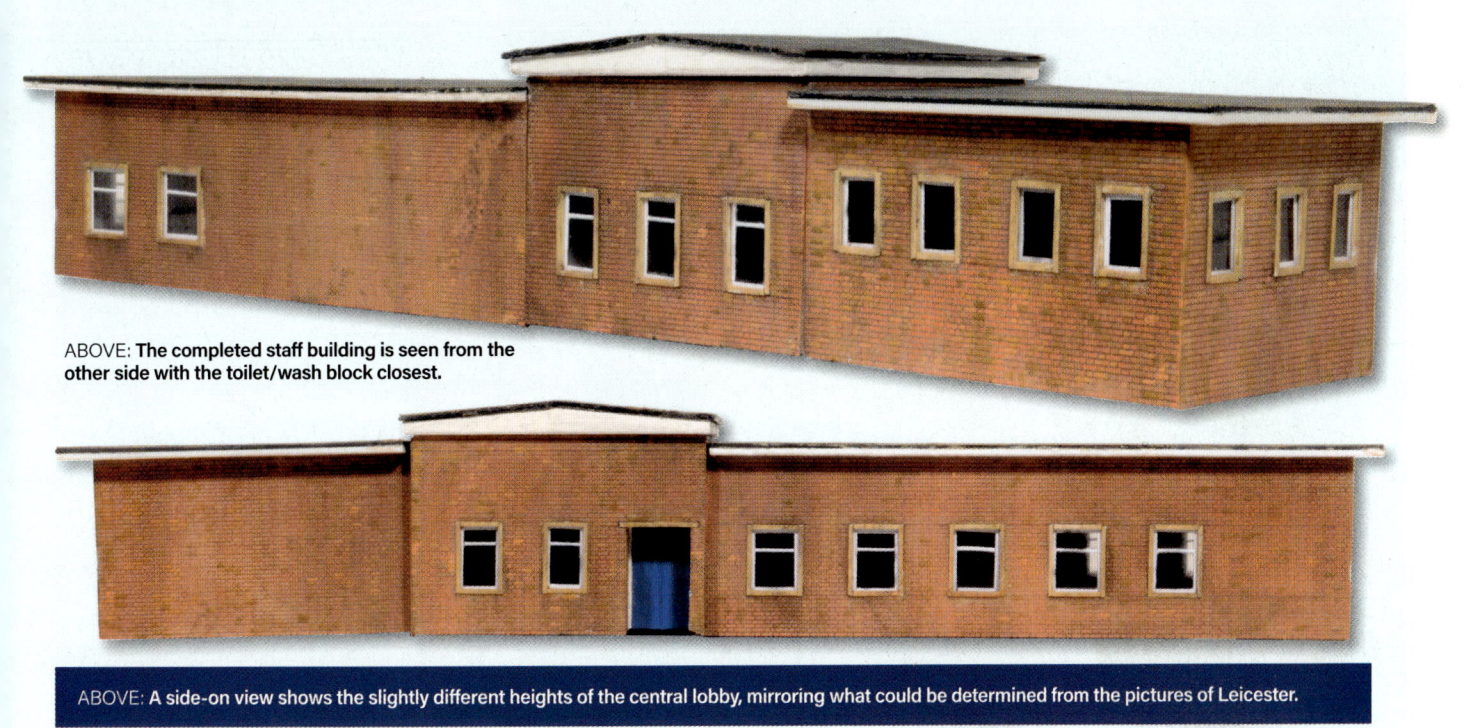

ABOVE: The completed staff building is seen from the other side with the toilet/wash block closest.

ABOVE: A side-on view shows the slightly different heights of the central lobby, mirroring what could be determined from the pictures of Leicester.

Modelling BR: Diesel Depots

Ancillary structures

Ready-to-plant options

ABOVE: The 1970s 'Prefab Commercial Building' is seen as supplied in the Scenecraft range.

Over the years, Bachmann's resin Scenecraft range has featured a number of moderately-sized structures that could all find a home on a stabling point or yard layout as staff accommodation. Those pictured here have all been in the 4mm scale range, but most have also appeared shrunken down to 2mm.

The first of interest is marketed as a Prefab Commercial Building (reference number 44-0070). This portrays one of the most common designs of prefabricated structure to emerge around the early 1970s, such buildings being found at schools and hospitals alongside commercial and leisure roles. British Rail made use of them as well within yards and depots, one example being at Tonbridge West Yard where the model is almost an exact match for the carriage and wagon staff bothy that once stood near the footbridge. The actual example modelled was found at March.

Externally it features a representative mix of panelling and wooden cladding and with a footprint of 128mm long by 57mm wide, it is a good size to occupy a corner of a layout from the 1970s to the 1990s. It was quite common for such prefab buildings to sit on a raised concrete base with steps up to the doors, which is something that can be added easily enough.

Modern pre-fab

Along similar lines is a modern version of a pre-fabricated building, this featuring a recent trend of having rendered walls (44-0094). Modelled as an 'L' shape, the longest walls measure 134mm by 94mm with a height of 46mm. Features include two doors with steps, a drainpipe and gutter, and moulded light. In railway terms, it could easily serve as a building for a relatively new or modernised depot or yard, having hints of the admin building at Gresty Bridge for example.

The rendered finish to the resin walls is particularly impressive while the rest of the decoration is a cut above as well, with the roof having a nice textured look and the windows generally being well fitted with little adjustment needed. All that is required externally is a bit of personalisation by adding signage and perhaps a few small details like extra lights.

The remaining photos on this page illustrate some of the other releases over the years, giving further variations on the same theme.

ABOVE: The modern day 'Rendered Prefab Building' is 'L'-shaped and well finished.

ABOVE: One of Bachmann's oldest Scenecraft release, the 'Office block' (44-039) featured on numerous layouts when first released, it measures 144mm by 64mm.

ABOVE: The 'Depot Crew Room' (44-0034) is another 'L'-shaped offering, its longest measurements being 158mm by 111mm.

ABOVE: The 'Shunters Mess Room' (44-139) measures 126mm by 81mm, with its suggested role being rather self-explanatory.

ABOVE: The most recent addition to this category is the 'Shunter's Hut' (44-0182), which is available with either white or blue paintwork and measures 80mm by 61mm.

Ancillary structures

Boiler houses

Many large BR era depots of a certain vintage had oil-fired boilers on the premises to provide heating. Even if these had fallen out of use in later years, the building often remained, complete with chimney.

RIGHT: The boiler house at Tinsley forms the backdrop to 56125 on an unrecorded date in the mid-1980s, this featuring a substantial chimney and its own oil storage tanks. The design mirrors the depot building by having a glass frontage. Simon Bendall Collection

BELOW LEFT AND BELOW RIGHT: The modern boiler building at Old Oak Common stood at the foot of the access road by the turntable, its contents being secreted away behind roller shutter doors. The rear is seen from across the turntable roads in April 2009, showing off the equally large chimney. Simon Bendall

BELOW AND RIGHT: The rear of the Factory building at Old Oak Common also contained a boiler house, this being directly behind 97804 in May 1986, the withdrawn Class 06 moving to the West London depot after the closure of Reading signal works. A peek around the internal door from 2008 shows the dormant boilers. Simon Bendall

Modelling BR: Diesel Depots 91

Ancillary structures

Building a boiler house by Terry Bendall

ABOVE: The completed boiler house kit ready for installation with a chimney from Bachmann's Scenecraft range as the finishing touch.

This boiler house is another Railway Laser Lines kit and is based on the one that was at Finsbury Park, although it is generic enough to be used in a number of situations. Once again, the kit consists of an internal shell with laser cut walls and other details but as a larger building, the number of components is considerably more than the pump house shown in the fuel tank section.

The shell consists of four walls with additional internal walls that include laser cut details, these being visible if clear windows and an interior are modelled. The supporting structure for the roof beams is quite fragile so care had to be taken when assembling the parts not to break anything, especially since it is a tight fit inside the basic box structure. Before any construction work began, the outside brick walls were sprayed with red oxide primer and the window frames and girders similarly airbrushed with grey primer. Both of these colours form a good starting point for subsequent painting.

Construction began by putting together the basic shell using PVA woodworking glue as the adhesive and with the floor fitted loosely inside to keep things square. Some long clamps were used to hold the shell together while the glue dried. The outside walls with the laser cut detail were then fitted, a trial fit being undertaken before gluing to ensure the corner joints of the brickwork bonding fitted tightly together. There is very little

ABOVE: The lower half of the boiler house is a basic box section with the shell clad in outer brick sheet. With the latter painted with red oxide before assembly, the box is seen from the rear after the mortar wash had been applied, again using Humbrol No.121.

tolerance in the fit and it may be necessary to either sand down the outside of the shell to get an accurate fit or apply filler afterwards to deal with any gaps in the corners. These were again fixed on using PVA and clamps.

Girder work

The next stage is to add the internal walls, which incorporate much of the roof girder work, and as these can be a tight fit, some slight trimming may be needed. This is best done using a sharp scalpel and a ruler, while PVA was again used to fix things in place with the aid of spring clamps. Once all the internal walls are in along with one

across the centre of the building, there are additional separate girders to fit across between them, these completing the roof supports.

The upper window frames are made from laser cut card with the glazing material designed to be sandwiched between the inner and outer frames. The clear glazing is supplied with a protective film applied, which can either be left in place to give an opaque look or be removed to allow the interior to be modelled and seen. In this case, the former won out.

The window frames were assembled using Deluxe Materials' Glue 'n' Glaze, which is ideal for this application since it

Ancillary structures

ABOVE: The next step in construction is to add the four internal wall sections along with the central cross-wall. These all incorporate parts of the roof structure and girders. Additional individual girders are then placed across the rest of the roof space to complete the structure, which are seen in the process of being fitted.

dries clear. The method used was to place one frame on a piece of scrap MDF about 12mm thick, apply small drops of adhesive to the frame using a cocktail stick, lay the glazing material in place and then place the second frame with adhesive added on top. A second piece of scrap MDF and some weights held everything together while the glue dried.

Topping off

While the window frames were drying, a further job was to fit the separate laser-cut door frames, which were painted white before being fixed in place. With the window assembles ready, any excess glazing material projecting from the edges of the frames was trimmed off and the top of the walls checked to make sure everything was level and free of dried glue.

The window assemblies were fitted one at a time on top of the walls using Glue 'n' Glaze and left to dry with spring clamps and some bulldog clips being used to hold them in place. Once the first frame had been fixed, masking tape was also used to hold the corners together while the glue dried.

The final large job for the building was to fit the roof and again abrasive paper was used to give a suitable finish, this being fixed in place and the roof panel then glued on top of the girders and window frames. Before fitting, a check was needed to make sure the roof would fit tightly all the way round and any excess material cleaned off before fixing. The last job was to paint all the doors, dark blue being the chosen colour in this case.

Mirroring a common arrangement for TMD boiler houses, a chimney was added. After another internet search, the 'Modern Industrial Chimney' (reference number 44-078) produced by Bachmann in its Scenecraft range some years ago was determined to be the best of the limited options available. One was duly found on eBay at a bit of a cost but was largely ready to use from the box and already suitably weathered. The only modification was to cut back the curved part of the joining pipe, allowing it to meet the boiler house wall square on. A new flange plate was made from plasticard with bolt detail added to give a suitable joint.

ABOVE: The modified pipe on the Scenecraft chimney with the scratchbuilt flange plate. Once installed on the layout, the baseplate for the chimney can be covered with scenery.

BELOW: The finished boiler house is quite an impressive sight and size with the opaque glazing being a nice touch. If the light hits it right, the outline of the roof beams can be seen behind it.

Modelling BR: Diesel Depots 93

Ancillary structures

LEFT: Opened in the early 2000s, the heavy repair facility at Old Oak Common was a brand new three-road shed built on part of the carriage sidings. It also included a stores area and road vehicle access doors, allowing components to be delivered and unloaded inside if required. Simon Bendall

Wheels and washes

Completing the look at ancillary depot facilities, **Simon Bendall** considers the equipment installed to deal with wheel and bogie maintenance as well as keeping the trains clean.

ABOVE: The centrepiece of the new building on opening was a bogie drop, this allowing a complete bogie to be removed and lowered from beneath a unit and lifted up onto the adjacent line. Once wheeled away, an overhauled bogie could then be put in place in the same manner. 180107 stands in front of the deep pit with the yellow bogie lift on the other road. Simon Bendall

ABOVE: An elevated walkway was also provided, specifically for the maintenance of roof-mounted air conditioning units on the Class 180s. Running down both sides of a coach length, this had hinged extensions to close the gap between the walkway and roof. 180112 sits beneath the gantry. Simon Bendall

LEFT: Outside of the new depot building, a wash facility was installed for cleaning bogies and underframes, this having side pits, extendable hoses, and splash screens down both sides. In the background is Great Western's servicing depot, then used for light maintenance and cleaning of HSTs and the Night Riviera sleeper stock. Simon Bendall

Ancillary structures

ABOVE: A more traditional wash plant is seen at Cardiff Canton as 37883 shunts along the depot access line on June 9, 1990. At some passenger stock depots, these washers were automatic but, in this case, it was manually activated by the driver if required. Bachmann has previously released a decent representation of a washer in the Scenecraft range. Simon Bendall Collection

ABOVE: Wheel lathes represent a considerable investment by companies but nowadays are a must-have item to prolong wheel life and deal with flat-spots before they become too severe. Around 1992, 47625 *Resplendent* is just that as it stands inside the wheel lathe building at Crewe Electric. Like a bogie drop, a deep pit is required to accommodate the lathe, which is a contributing factor to their high installation cost. Simon Bendall Collection

ABOVE: As rolling stock undergoing tyre turning is not normally moved under its own power, many depots equipped with a lathe have a small battery shunter to shuffle backwards and forwards on the lathe road. Such vehicles have also become popular for general shunting at some locations in place of the venerable Class 08 with larger and more powerful variants available than those pictured here. Niteq is a major supplier of these machines with a 5000-E series seen on GWR's side of Old Oak Common on September 2, 2017. Others are radio-controlled as per this example at Northampton Kings Heath on December 11, 2017. Simon Bendall

LEFT: It is rare to see a wheel lathe portrayed in model form, but Aberdeen Kirkhill by Glenn Daniel and Graham Harris is an exception, it provides some additional operational interest on the ScotRail depot set in the late 1980s. This was positioned at the far end of Kirkhill depot along with the wash plant and toilet tank discharge area, with 47578 *The Royal Society of Edinburgh* seen going for a spin. Dennis Taylor

Modelling BR: Diesel Depots 95

Ancillary structures

Water tanks

Many would doubtless be surprised to still find a large capacity water tank provided at many TMDs, such structures being associated with steam operation. However, even a diesel depot still needs a water supply to replenish locos and carry out some operations as Simon Bendall explains.

ABOVE: While many TMDs had a steel water tank, Tinsley was different, having a pre-cast round concrete version instead. This stood at the north end of the depot, adjacent to the throat and opposite the fuel storage tanks on the other side of the line. On October 10, 1997, the Railfreight Distribution pairing of 47309 *The Halewood Transmission* and 47213 *Marchwood Military Port* are prominent as the water tank competes with the lighting towers to see which is the tallest structure around. Also on depot was 47033 *The Royal Logistics Corps*, this standing near a wagon chassis adapted to carry a Class 47 engine roof panel. Storing removed roof panels was a problem at several depots, a number using wagons to carry them. At Toton, the mid-1990s saw brackets devised that could clip into the cantrail grilles on a Class 56, these holding the roof panel above the rest of the loco at one end. Railfreight Distribution would be sold to EWS at the end of 1997, sealing the fate of Tinsley, which was closed five months after this picture was taken with demolition underway by the end of 1998. Simon Bendall Collection

ABOVE: While depots typically had their redundant steam era infrastructure demolished after 1968, bits and pieces could still be seen beyond those steam sheds that survived in whole or in part. For example, the stabling point at Ranelagh Bridge retained its water tower following the takeover of diesel traction. On an unrecorded date in 1979, 47500 *Great Western* stands with a sister by the fuel tankers. The view from those windows must have been either glorious or appalling depending on your interests! Simon Bendall Collection

Ancillary structures

ABOVE: **The Toton water tank was of more modern construction than those illustrated below at Old Oak Common, being formed of sheet steel in comparison to the pressed panels. Still standing today, it forms the backdrop to 58035 by the fuelling point on July 24, 1994. Like its classmates, it was now under the ownership of Trainload Freight South East so had seen the removal of its Trainload Coal sub-sector emblems. New Mainline Freight logos would not be applied until the following year.** Simon Bendall Collection

ABOVE: **Old Oak Common had two water tanks on the depot, the larger one standing near the traincrew mess and above the covered stores area. This is the one on which the model overleaf is based. The stores in this area tended to be large, bulky items with some positioned under the canopy, including a pallet full of bags of loco sand. Also under there is a diesel-powered forklift while the loco wheelsets on their transport cradles are left in the open.** Simon Bendall

BELOW: **A closer view of the water tank atop its supporting frame in September 2008 with the distinctive pressed steel panels succumbing to a lack of maintenance. Eight cross-members support the tank with a variety of pipes feeding into the bottom of it. The ladder and safety cage are at the other end.** Simon Bendall

ABOVE: **The other water tank at Old Oak Common, seen in December 2008, was taller, both in support structure and the actual tank, but squarer. This was of more modern construction with a girder framework and a three-piece ladder with two intermediate landings. Three pipes run vertically all the way to the ground with a couple more joining together beneath the tank. In the distance are the depot entry and exit roads.** Simon Bendall

Modelling BR: Diesel Depots

Ancillary structures

Scratchbuilding a depot water tank by Terry Bendall

ABOVE: The basis of the tank is a styrene box which is then clad in the pressed steel panels taken from the Wills water tower kit. For this tank, four packs were needed to make the sides and ends with the leftovers going underneath along with a few scratchbuilt examples to make up the numbers as it was getting a bit expensive!

When looking at how the water tank could be created, it was found that there was nothing really suitable as a ready to plant item and very few kits available. The Wills steam-era water tank kit (SS34), while otherwise unsuitable, did include the pressed steel panels with their distinctive 'x' shape so one of these was purchased to see if the parts could form the basis of a scratchbuilt tank.

These investigations proved positive so three more kits were acquired to get sufficient panels to do all four sides and much of the underneath as well. Scratchbuilding models from brass is something that I enjoy so the legs and supporting frame did not present a problem. With one of the tanks at Old Oak Common serving as the inspiration, sizes were estimated from pictures, using adjacent structures as reference points.

Construction started with the tank and the first job was to make a styrene box from 40 thou black plastic to which the steel panels could be fixed. With the sides completed, the underneath was then tackled. However, there were not quite enough panels left over to fully cover the area but, rather than buy an additional kit from which much of it would go straight in the bin, a few additional panels were made up from styrene. These came out reasonably well but were located on the corners, where the supporting frame would help obscure their slightly different look.

Adding a roof

It was unclear from photos if the Old Oak tank had a roof but determining from other depot water tanks that it most likely did, one was added anyway. This was made from styrene sheet to represent welded sheet steel, with the plastic scored to represent the weld joints

LEFT: The support for the tank is also made from brass 'I' section of two different sizes.

ABOVE: One of the pair of legs is seen after construction was completed, it being entirely made of brass from channel section, sheet offcuts and wire for the diagonal bracing.

Ancillary structures

cross-members, these again being soldered together. While solder of different melting points can be used so that joints made first do not fall apart when later joints are formed, I usually manage with using solder of the same melting point throughout, although small pieces of wood are very useful to hold things in place while subsequent joints are made.

Braces all round
Once the legs and frame were made, they were assembled using a lower melting point solder with an engineer's try-square being used to make sure the corners were at right angles. The cross-braces between each pair of legs were made from 2mm by 1.5mm 'I' section brass, while the diagonal tie-braces were made from 0.7mm brass wire with small squares of brass sheet being used to represent the joint in the middle.

The ladder and safety cage were from the Walthers range and, although a little crude being plastic, they had been kicking about in the spares box for years so were finally put to a good use. In addition, etched safety cages are rather hard to come by. At the top of the ladder, an access platform was made from 1.5mm brass angle and 0.45mm brass wire, being glued to the side of the tank.

The base and tank were then airbrushed separately to allow access all round to paint with Humbrol No.28 grey. When happy with the finish, the two were glued together and weathered, largely using washes of Railmatch sleeper grime.

ABOVE: With construction of the main sections completed, they were placed together to get an impression of how the model would look and to check everything was square and level.

and then stuck in position. The last job on the tank was to add an access hatch, which was made from a small square of 10 thou brass sheet with a hinge from 0.45mm brass wire and a handle from 0.3mm brass wire.

Construction of the supports began with the legs, which were made from 3mm x 2mm brass channel section joined with plates made from 20 thou brass sheet, all being soldered together. The latter came from my box of scrap etch which is a very useful source of small pieces of sheet.

The tank support frame used brass 'I' section material with 5mm by 2mm being employed for the longitudinal parts and 3mm by 2mm for the

ABOVE: Detail additions to the tank were the access hatch in the roof along with the adjacent platform at the top of the ladder, these both being made from brass and seen following painting.

ABOVE: The completed water tank following the addition of the Walthers ladder and safety cage assembly, the angled positioning mirroring that of the Old Oak one. The model has also been weathered. Once installed on the layout, the water feed pipes down to the ground will be added.

Modelling BR: Diesel Depots **99**

Ancillary structures

Turntable survivors

Completing the examination of depot infrastructure, Simon Bendall takes a quick look at turntables, which were another steam era feature that still lived on in some locations.

ABOVE: St Blazey was host to 50017 *Royal Oak* on July 24, 1982, more than two years after it became the second Class 50 to be released from refurbishment at Doncaster Works. One of the six to be outshopped in BR blue, an application of large logo was still a year and a half away. The turntable at the Cornish depot was retained out of necessity as it gave access to the nine-road roundhouse, this surviving until closed by EWS in 1997, after which all maintenance was carried out in the former wagon shop. The roundhouse building was later converted into industrial units and fenced off from the turntable but still stands today. The turntable itself eventually fell into despair until refurbished by Network Rail early in 2023, solely for the use of steam specials working to the area. Simon Bendall Collection

ABOVE: Once home to four interconnected turntables, Old Oak Common retained just one after conversion to diesel servicing, this giving access to a number of lines used for loco stabling, as well as for the depot's snowploughs. However, with the HST depot next door, the turntable could also be called upon to turn power cars and this was taking place on an unrecorded date in 1990 with 43124. The turntable remained in use until the final months of the depot in the spring of 2009 and was donated to the Swanage Railway when demolition began. Simon Bendall Collection

RIGHT: HSTs were the reason that turntables were retained at a handful of other depots involved in their upkeep, including Neville Hill and Bristol Bath Road. The latter is seen in October 1993, it being sited near the depot entrance. The depot would close in 1995 with HST work transferring the short distance to St Philip's Marsh, after which power cars were turned by sending them on a triangular tour of local lines. In contrast, the turntable at Neville Hill was still there in September 2023, but now largely redundant with the demise of the CrossCountry HST fleet. Simon Bendall Collection

100 www.keymodelworld.com

VISIT OUR ONLINE SHOP
TO VIEW OUR FULL RANGE OF SPECIAL MAGAZINES ABOUT **MODEL RAIL AND THE INDUSTRY**

Key Shop

shop.keypublishing.com/specials

£8.99 — This eagerly awaited follow up to the popular Modelling British Railways series traces the development of the many diesel and electric classes through the decade as they transitioned from BR to private ownership.

£8.99 — In this highly anticipated follow up to his Greatest Layouts special published in 2022, Pete Waterman and the Railnuts group are taking on their biggest challenge yet.

£8.99 — This new publication will show how to model a range of locomotives across two decades and in various scales while considering the numerous freight companies that have existed during this period.

£8.99 — This publication will look at all the types used for ballast, sleeper and rail carrying over this period along with their operations and train formations.

£8.99 — In this highly anticipated follow up to his Greatest Layouts special published in 2022, Pete Waterman and the Railnuts group are taking on their biggest challenge yet.

£9.99 — Hornby Magazine presents the fourth volume of its popular Great Layouts series bringing together some of the very best model railways to have ever featured in the magazine.

£8.99 — As well as reflecting of the successes of 2022, such as the opening of Crossrail and progress with HS2, the expert editorial team attempts to chart the likely way forward for the year to come.

£9.99 — Rail 123 is the only publication to list ALL vehicles in one easy to follow, colour coded list. The new edition of Rail 123 includes more than 20,000 changes and updates from the 2021-2022 edition.

FREE P&P* when you order online at...
shop.keypublishing.com/specials

Call **+44 (0)1780 480404** (Monday to Friday 9am-5.30pm GMT)

Also available from **W.H Smith** and all leading newsagents. Or download from **Pocketmags.com** or your native app store - search *Aviation Specials*

SUBSCRIBERS don't forget to use your **£2 OFF DISCOUNT CODE!**

*Free 2nd class P&P on all UK & BFPO orders. Overseas charges apply.

Ancillary structures

Two loco-length inspection platforms are provided at the north end of DRS' Carlisle Kingmoor depot, these being fixed structures. During the open day on July 7, 2007, 47237 was stabled between them. PH Designs offers an etched kit for just such a permanent installation, this measuring 170mm in length and with steps provided at one end. *Simon Bendall*

Depot equipment

Having considered an array of subjects related to depot buildings, it is now time for **Simon Bendall** to explore all the equipment and fittings that populated these structures for use in maintaining locos and to see what is available in model form.

Clutter, for want of a better collective term, is what brings a depot layout to life, this encompassing everything from access steps and oil drums to depot signage and forklift trucks, with a lot more in between. While it is possible to add too many items to a depot building, particularly a smaller one, there is typically all manner of stuff lying about as the following few pages will attempt to show.

Many of these items lend themselves to 3D printing so it is no surprise to see a host of useful bits and pieces listed in the ranges of the likes of West Hill Wagon Works, Goodwood Scenics, Rusty Rails Modelling, and 3D Printing Corner. There are also firms like Scale Model Scenery, Ten Commandments, PH Designs and S Kits that offer items in an assortment of materials. A selection of kits and details are also illustrated here to give a flavour of what is available, but it is well worth checking out the various websites to see the complete ranges.

ABOVE: The portable inspection gantry is a common sight at many depots and while they differ in details and colours, the basic design is the same. This includes steps at one end, a platform more or less level with solebar height and with a railing on one side and the other end, and some sort of handbrake. This galvanised version recorded at Gresty Bridge on March 11, 2014, was being used alongside 20302. A step ladder is alongside, although these do not seem as common in a depot environment as you might think. *Simon Bendall*

ABOVE: A gantry on a gantry at Kingmoor on July 16, 2011, in order to reach the cantrail of 37601. The stand alongside to hold the 'Not to be moved' boards is a neat idea, these being the style that fit over a lamp bracket and protrude out to the side at an angle. Different companies have different requirements for these, including magnetic designs and ones with integrated flashing red lights. Chocks with handles sit on top of the blue cabinet; a depot can never have too many chocks! *Simon Bendall*

Ancillary structures

ABOVE: Looking back at the British Rail era, a diverse range of steps was evident as well. 40015 leads 25132 and an unidentified Class 47 at Wigan Springs Branch on December 14, 1980, with 40191 on the other road. Two different heights of step are evident while a scaffolding tower looms over the 'Brush 4' with a work platform incorporated at cantrail height. Simon Bendall Collection

ABOVE: A short, fixed inspection platform accommodates 08865 inside Cambridge depot during 1991 with a DMU car alongside. Some depot's had a small foreman's office inside the main building, with one visible beyond the drum racking. From the state of it, the black trolley may well be an oil pump. Simon Bendall Collection

ABOVE: A taller than normal portable gantry is seen at Toton in 2007 alongside 60073 *Cairn Gorm* to give cantrail access. Further down, there is portable welding equipment. Simon Bendall Collection

ABOVE: The 'daddy' of access ladders is seen employed on 56054 at Thornaby around 1994. Designed to give roof access from ground level, the type incorporated a handrail and typically had rubber feet on the flat platform at the top to give purchase on the loco roof. Somewhat difficult to manoeuvre into place, they are not for the faint hearted! Simon Bendall Collection

ABOVE: Ten Commandments offers an etched brass kit for a typical portable inspection platform in 4mm, this formerly being part of the Peter Clark range. Somewhat fiddly to assemble, it needs to be glued or soldered together as it is folded up. The platform is also available fully built and painted but at a price. This is the kit version, assembled with care and then painted, red being a common colour for these.

ABOVE: Goodwood Scenics offers two types of portable gantry in 4mm with differing platform lengths, the shorter one being typically used for loco cab access while the longer style is a working platform. These are supplied ready built in packs of two and available in a range of colours. A 7mm version is also offered.

Modelling BR: Diesel Depots 103

Ancillary structures

ABOVE: The controlled and safe movement of locos around a depot has always been important, although depot mishaps were far from infrequent during BR days. Signage plays a part in this, and Tinsley displays the common 'Stop Await instructions' boards on the approach to the fuelling points and shed doors in October 1995. On shed are 47157 and 47296, the latter having recently received new Railfreight Distribution logos to replace its obsolete Petroleum ones. Simon Bendall Collection

ABOVE: Depots often had local styles of signage to suit their particular situations as illustrated at Old Oak Common on October 11, 2008, the road off the turntable being signed 'Stop Ensure crossing is clear and sound horn before proceeding'. A warning sign for road vehicles is positioned just behind, while hinged barriers are also provided but long out of use. Simon Bendall

ABOVE: Depot protection equipment has become increasingly important over the last 30 years or so to manage risks, with many locations now having hinged chocks or de-railers protecting depot doors. Old Oak Common employed the chock style outside the Factory, this requiring a pin to be removed before it would hinge down.

ABOVE: Equally common is the de-railer, which will do as described if run over by a loco. These are invariably accompanied by a combined stop sign and lamp in the four foot, as seen at Gresty Bridge. The concrete sections immediately behind the sign are covering a cable run beneath the rails.

ABOVE: Like the chock, the de-railer folds down with the securing pin removed as does the stop sign. At some locations, like Eastleigh Works, the depot protection is electrically linked to an alarm so as soon as it is lowered, this sounds continuously.

ABOVE: The 'Not to be moved' boards at Gresty Bridge may not be depot protection as such but they are difficult to miss, sitting between the rails. These are usually found by the road crossing in front of the stabled locos on either side and would be easy to make in 4mm.

Ancillary structures

ABOVE: From a time before the all-prevailing palisade fencing, the entrance to Tyseley is seen in the early 1990s with a Centro logo added to the sign. The wagons look inviting for photography while 40118 and 50043 reside in the Birmingham Railway Museum.

ABOVE: Equally low key is the gateway to Bescot TMD, sited at the bottom of a short slope from a residential street. 37049 *Imperial* stands at the rear of the depot building alongside some of the horizontal fuel storage tanks in their red oxide colouring.

ABOVE: A more professional approach to depot signage is seen at Laira, Plymouth, in the early 1990s, the depot going so far as to create a viewing area from which proceedings could be observed, Good luck getting any depot to do that today!

ABOVE: Some depots delineate the boundary from which staff must have personal track safety certification and the associated safety clothing, as at Gresty Bridge. This is necessary as some facilities will have none-rail staff on site for administration roles.

ABOVE: The depot signage at Gresty Bridge on the side of the maintenance building, including the typical mix of direction and health and safety signs. The security level one is somewhat unusual though, presumably relating to the company's principal traffic.

LEFT: More safety signage on a personal door at Kingmoor, this one reminding staff to wear safety boots and warning of forklifts in operation. A light and warning stripes on the floor complete a fairly typical shed scene.

RIGHT: With the staff walking route at Old Oak Common passing across the front of the servicing shed, a large stop board was provided to remind people to check the crossing was clear, this being backed up by a light. An older 'Danger Beware of moving locomotives' sign is mounted on the depot wall alongside.

Ancillary structures

LEFT: Bounds Green appears to have an excess of drums, both metal and plastic, on November 12, 1988, as they are lined up alongside 89001. A number of companies offer oil drums across the three main scales in a variety of mediums. Behind the prototype AC electric are two former BR fish vans relegated to internal use while the Mk.2 behind the loco is an HST barrier coach, these being commonly found at both Eastern and Western InterCity depots maintaining the fleet. *Simon Bendall Collection*

RIGHT: Cardiff Canton was also host to a number of drums on June 20, 1992, these being less numerous but more colourful. All are laid on stands and labelled as to their contents. Depot mascot 56044 *Cardiff Canton* was looking a bit grimy behind, it keeps company with 60025. An early version of the stop boards protecting the depot doors are already in use in front of the locos. *Simon Bendall Collection*

LEFT: The roundhouse at Barrow Hill was still nine years from closure on March 26, 1982, as 20112 slumbers inside. A variety of portable gantries can be seen on the far side of the shed while, with the depot also responsible for wagon maintenance, spare wagon wheels are lined up on one of the roads alongside the turntable. West Hill Wagon Works offers 3D printed wheels of both loco and wagon types to populate a depot, the loco ones being easy to discern as they would feature a gear on the axle to fit the traction motors. *Simon Bendall Collection*

Ancillary structures

LEFT: Following transfer from ScotRail to Network SouthEast, a yet to be debranded 47701 was stabled at Old Oak Common in mid-1991 alongside withdrawn 50039. The interest comes in the freshly overhauled and palletised DMU engines alongside, along with the two Class 08 wheelsets lying on the gravel. The Class 47/7 would receive NSE colours that August and be named after the West London depot. *Simon Bendall Collection*

RIGHT: Dozens of spent batteries litter the ground at Laira in the early 1990s as two more withdrawn Class 50s, this time 50040 and 50010, await their date with the scrapman. Loco batteries are heavy things, so it is no surprise to see them on pallets or crated to allow ease of handling. To the right, fresh drums have been delivered with shrink wrapping still on them. *Simon Bendall Collection*

LEFT: Loco maintenance was still ongoing at Old Oak Common in March 2009 as preserved 50026 *Indomitable* receives attention. In the foreground is a brake test trolley, it being connected to the loco's bufferbeam pipes to run a test on the brake pressure available. Meanwhile, barrels of oil are being pumped into the engine following its re-fitting after overhaul, this being achieved via the pump on the trolley and the hose passing through the cab door and then through the radiator compartment. *Simon Bendall*

Modelling BR: Diesel Depots

Ancillary structures

ABOVE: The intermediate bulk containers are now as common at depots as oil drums used to be, these holding all manner of liquids from fuel and oil to cleaning detergents. The style varies but a plastic container inside a lightweight alloy frame is the standard.

ABOVE: Although looking nondescript, these boxes contain thousands of pounds of electronics in the form of GSM-R digital radios waiting for installation into DRS locos back in 2012 at Gresty Bridge, each one being lettered for a specific class or sub-class.

ABOVE: A pair of spare Class 67 bogies were recorded among the wheelsets at Old Oak Common in 2008, with a pair of wheel-less Class 58 bogie frames stacked up behind them. Fertis-liveried 56060 was also awaiting removal from the depot.

ABOVE: To allow for the easy and safe movement of wheelsets by forklifts, wheel cradles tend to be used nowadays, these also acting as chocks when on the ground. Class 67 wheelsets with their distinctive disc brake faces are seen at Old Oak.

ABOVE: Several manufacturers now offer models of small anonymous plastic tanks that can sit in a corner of a depot, including from the Bachmann range. This pair were recorded at Merehead atop breeze block supports alongside the depot building.

ABOVE: Typical of the clutter to be found at a depot, this selection at Gresty Bridge includes a battery charger, an oil drum in use as a bin alongside the plastic equivalent, and sundry other bits. The red drum on the wall is a reeled, compressed air hose.

LEFT: Different types of brake block lie outside Kingmoor on pallets, this including the modern composite type alongside the traditional steel version, the latter being easy to discern thanks to the rust. These are one of the biggest consumables at a depot.

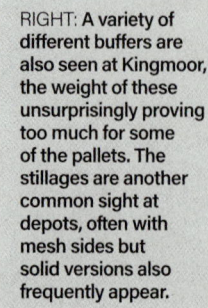

RIGHT: A variety of different buffers are also seen at Kingmoor, the weight of these unsurprisingly proving too much for some of the pallets. The stillages are another common sight at depots, often with mesh sides but solid versions also frequently appear.

Ancillary structures

RIGHT: A number of different manufacturers now offer the IBCs in model form in 4mm scale, Bachmann being one of the first in its Scenecraft depot accessories pack that also included batteries and brake blocks moulded in black plastic to go on pallets. Some of the nicest IBCs are available from Goodwood Scenics, which are supplied fully finished with a choice of lid colours. Even better, they are offered in bulk packs to rapidly fill your depot or yard. The tank is just a push fit inside the cage so can be removed if desired to leave the odd empty frame lying about.

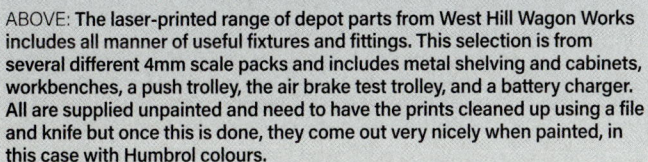

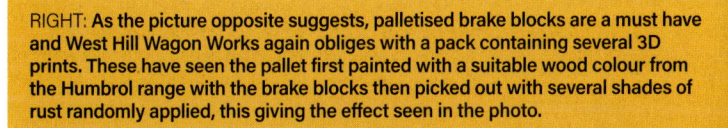

ABOVE: The laser-printed range of depot parts from West Hill Wagon Works includes all manner of useful fixtures and fittings. This selection is from several different 4mm scale packs and includes metal shelving and cabinets, workbenches, a push trolley, the air brake test trolley, and a battery charger. All are supplied unpainted and need to have the prints cleaned up using a file and knife but once this is done, they come out very nicely when painted, in this case with Humbrol colours.

RIGHT: As the picture opposite suggests, palletised brake blocks are a must have and West Hill Wagon Works again obliges with a pack containing several 3D prints. These have seen the pallet first painted with a suitable wood colour from the Humbrol range with the brake blocks then picked out with several shades of rust randomly applied, this giving the effect seen in the photo.

ABOVE: Finally from the West Hill range is a pack containing traction motors and gear wheels, some of which are moulded on pallets. These are very nicely printed with plenty of surface detail and look impressive when cleaned up and painted. Other much larger loco components are also available, including complete bogies and power units from different classes, which could either be blocked up on a depot floor or added to a flat wagon as described in the next section.

Modelling BR: Diesel Depots 109

Internal users

Internal users

Many depots made use of wagons and occasionally coaches for storing an assortment of supplies and materials as well as moving components around the sites. These were known as internal users and, under BR, normally numbered in their own series. David Ratcliffe **and** Simon Bendall **look at some examples.**

Under British Rail, numerous wagons found a second career once they had been withdrawn from main line service, ending up in internal service at depots, yards, freight terminals and the like. Once transferred to such use, they were restricted to that location and were not to leave without special permission as all scheduled maintenance ceased.

Their uses could be diverse but, for those at depots, vans were typically used to hold all manner of stores, such as bags of loco sand and other consumables, while tankers were useful for storing waste oil until it was periodically removed by a road tanker. Flat and well wagons of assorted types could be loaded with engines, bogies, and other large components to move them around depots, to road transport or sometimes as mobile work platforms. Coaches, particularly former parcels vans, were also useful as stores vehicles although less common, while other roles could include classrooms, additional office space and similar. Many internal users were typically static in their new roles, but others could be shunted around as required.

All vehicles transferred to internal use were meant to be assigned and carry a new identity, these six digit numbers being divided up into five regional series. On the London Midland Region, they were in the 02xxxx series, Eastern 04xxxx, Western 06xxxx and occasionally 07xxxx, Southern 08xxxx and finally in Scotland 09xxxx. Numbers were generally allocated as intended but carrying them was more hit and miss. Vehicles that found themselves grounded for a new role at a depot were normally not included in the internal series, although there were exceptions, and these were considered as withdrawn and disposed of for stock control purposes.

Upon privatisation in 1994, the internal user numbering system was abandoned and the number of vehicles finding such a role plummeted as supplies of suitable wagons and coaches dried up and the number of depots decreased. However, some stock still found new uses, these either retaining their existing number or not displaying one at all. Today, the number of internal users is much reduced as surplus shipping containers and lightweight storage tanks have taken over many of the tasks. There are though still examples to be found along with a few grounded bodies.

Depots were often also home to other stock from the departmental coaches and wagons fleets. This included breakdown cranes and their support coaches, snowploughs and, in BR days at least, stores vans and tankers. Many of these subjects have featured in volume five of the *Modelling British Railways* series, which covered various categories of departmental coaches and track machines, but a few additional images are included here.

ABOVE: A number of former six-wheel milk tanks found their way into internal service, often being used to hold waste oil. During the summer of 1987, ADW3035 and ADW44044, the latter still displaying traces of its St Ivel livery, are pumped out into a road tanker at Bristol Bath Road. The waste oil would be reprocessed to produce a useable fuel oil. The 'Not to be used for milk' lettering seems a mite redundant! Trevor Mann Collection

RIGHT: At Chester, Medfit DB460675 was used to carry refuse, such as old pallets and plastic sheeting, from the TMD to the adjacent National Carriers sidings where it could more easily be loaded into a bin lorry for disposal. Allocated internal number 024514 and lettered 'For internal use only TMD Dept. Chester', the former ZAO was recorded at Chester on May 2, 1994. David Ratcliffe

Internal users

ABOVE: Lowmacs and similar well wagons were used to move large items around at several depots, such a shunt being demonstrated at Bristol Bath Road in the early 1990s as 08643 manoeuvres an unidentified Lowmac. This is carrying two HST power car cooler groups, one freshly overhauled and the other in ex traffic condition. Under BR's maintenance policy at the time, components were often removed and sent away for overhaul to a main workshop with a fresh example taking its place. *Simon Bendall Collection*

ABOVE: Some wagons were adapted for their internal roles such as BR 20-ton brake van ADB952647, which had its bodywork removed so the chassis could carry a 'sludge gulper' to clean out catch pits and drains at Neville Hill depot in Leeds. Although devoid of its internal identity 041450, it is lettered 'Not to leave Neville Hill' and 'Depot use only'. Recorded on October 12, 1997, it is still at the depot in 2023. *Trevor Mann*

ABOVE: Never given an internal user number, Lowmac DE278497 has served as an HST power car engine carrier at Neville Hill for over 30 years, it also being recorded on October 12, 1997. Wagons employed as engine carriers invariably had a modified floor with raised blocks, these being arranged to accommodate the mounting feet and sump of the engine, which was then bolted down. Railings and similar sometimes also featured for safety reasons. *David Ratcliffe*

RIGHT: A third member of the internal user fleet at Neville Hill is 041901, this being former 'Condor' bogie Conflat B510001. Again pictured in October 1997 but still there in 2023, it is used to transfer heavy components around the depot, having been recorded carrying HST power car cooler groups, engine stands, lifting beams and similar. *David Ratcliffe*

Modelling BR: Diesel Depots 111

Internal users

ABOVE: A number of vacuum-braked vans ended their days as internal users at TMDs, including BR insulated meat van B872042. As 041421, it is seen in November 1986 at Immingham TMD, where it was used as an equipment store. David Ratcliffe

ABOVE: Repainted in unmistakable fashion, 041498, formerly BR 12-ton Vanfit B786181, is seen at Neville Hill on October 12, 1997. This van was donated to the Quorn Wagon and Wagon group in 2020 and restored as part of its collection. Trevor Mann

ABOVE: Former BR shocvan ADB854308 was employed as a static stores van, complete with access steps, at Pantyffynnon for many years, being used to hold bags of sand for replenishing locomotive sandboxes. Seen on September 16, 1981. Simon Bendall Collection

ABOVE: An example of a 12-ton van transferred to departmental use to deliver stores to depots, ADB785806 was recorded at Haymarket on September 27, 1981. It is lettered 'Loco material only Haymarket TMD 04230' and 'CM&EE Haymarket'. Simon Bendall Collection

ABOVE: Grounded 12-ton vans were once a common sight at depots and yards. Pictured on September 30, 1981, B768823 had ended its days at Ayr TMD, the provision of a concrete access ramp being a little more out of the ordinary. Simon Bendall Collection

ABOVE: The majority of grounded vans were left in as withdrawn condition but occasionally a repaint would be carried out. With its original identity obliterated, a diagram 1/209 shocvan was at Hamilton depot on September 28, 1981. Simon Bendall Collection

ABOVE: A number of air-braked vans, particularly VDAs, found their way into internal use when their revenue careers were prematurely cut short by traffic losses. Carrying InterCity colours, 200663 was employed at St Philip's Marsh when seen on May 2, 2016. Simon Bendall

ABOVE: Something of an upgrade from a 12-ton van, Mk.1 Super BG 94498 was one of two redundant roller shutter mail vans transferred to internal use at Toton by EWS. Repainted in blue, it is still at the depot in 2023 but now kept outside. Simon Bendall Collection

Internal users

LEFT: **08708 stands at Colchester in December 1991 with ADB701441, otherwise known as 042177, the former Conflat A having been modified to carry a square tank to hold waste oil. This would be periodically tripped over to the yard to allow for emptying into a road tanker, disposal coming in the early 1990s after the depot was closed.** Simon Bendall Collection

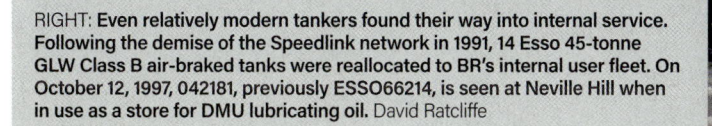

RIGHT: **Even relatively modern tankers found their way into internal service. Following the demise of the Speedlink network in 1991, 14 Esso 45-tonne GLW Class B air-braked tanks were reallocated to BR's internal user fleet. On October 12, 1997, 042181, previously ESSO66214, is seen at Neville Hill when in use as a store for DMU lubricating oil.** David Ratcliffe

ABOVE: **Former Shell Mex/BP anchor-mounted 20-ton tank 6265, which was built by Turner in 1948, had become 024478 when pictured at Machynlleth DMU refuelling point on July 28, 1984.** Trevor Mann

ABOVE: **Also seen at Machynlleth on July 28, 1984 was 023215, this being a former Midland Railway 10-ton tank. Several ancient wagons survived for a lengthy period of time in internal use.** Trevor Mann

ABOVE: **Seen at Exeter Riverside on May 1, 1993, former GWR twin-barrel tank W2564W became ADW150141 after its transfer to the departmental fleet for use in weedkilling trains. Subsequently, it became 070882 at Exmouth Junction for fuel oil storage.** Hywel Thomas

ABOVE: **Diagram DD6 water tank ADW103 is seen at Cardiff Canton on July 11, 1982, with traces of its old 'Loco Dept water tank drinking water' lettering still just about discernible at the far end of the barrel. However, it was now in use as a sludge storage tank.** Hywel Thomas

Modelling BR: Diesel Depots 113

Internal users

ABOVE: Under EWS/DB ownership, a number of former civil engineers flat wagons have found themselves restricted to depot only duties, these all retaining their existing identities following the demise of the internal user numbering system. Recorded at Old Oak Common on August 30, 2008, YMA Salmon DB996496 was one such example, it carrying a Class 66 bogie frame and a power unit stand amongst other things. As it was in restricted use, it missed out on receiving replacement ASF bogies like many of its classmates, retaining the 8ft long plate bogies. *Simon Bendall*

ABOVE: Six-axle Weltrol EJC ADB901200 was the first of six wagons built in 1964 to diagram 2/750. Originally rated at 55-tons, the Class 66 bogie frame would hardly have taxed it when recorded at Old Oak Common on September 13, 2008. Coded YVW, its days of working to the continent via the train ferry were long over. Stored Fertis-liveried 58016 stands behind, this surviving today in preservation. *Simon Bendall*

ABOVE: The Bristol Bath Road breakdown crane, believed to be ADRR95213, stands outside the administration block at the depot around 1980. A Ransomes & Rapier 45-ton steam crane, it is accompanied by its water tanker, runners, and an open wagon for carrying packing material. Under BR, breakdown cranes were kept at main depots where traction and staff were readily available if needed. *Simon Bendall Collection*

RIGHT: The Eastfield breakdown crane support coaches are seen on the Glasgow depot on June 2, 1976, consisting of a mix of LNER and BR designs. Nearest the camera is tool coach ADE320691, a heavily rebuilt Gresley brake third corridor, this being scrapped in November 1984. *Simon Bendall Collection*